Mind Y'self Now, Jewarne

MIND Y'SELF NOW, JEWARNE

A Kiwi in Donegal & Dublin

JOANNE DOHERTY

To dear Helen & Kevin
My very first copy
is for you!
It is full of love &
thanks for your
friendship & support.
See you in
September.
Joanne

May
2008.

STEELE ROBERTS
AOTEAROA NEW ZEALAND

Dedicated to Myles, Bridget, John, Catherine, Bernard, Elizabeth, John and Mary from the clans of McPaddens, Clunes, Roddens, McElwains, Dohertys, Whelans, Kirwans and Phelans. They danced at the crossroads in Donegal, Clare, Fermanagh, Leitrim and Waterford before their journeys to Aotearoa New Zealand.

© Joanne Doherty 2008
Poems and photos are by Joanne unless otherwise credited.

www.JoanneDoherty.co.nz

The cover photo by Joanne Doherty is a backdrop to this tale: Jack Doherty and Margaret Kelly, cousins meeting at the Grianán of Aileach, the ancient ring fort in Inishowen, land of the O'Dochartaigh clan.

Author photo: Roze Doherty. The Celtic design 'In Continuum' on the back cover & page 1 is by Stephen King. In Irish tradition the shamrock represents the Holy Trinity; the four-leaf shamrock in this book represents God's grace, and is a Celtic symbol of good luck. Production: Marie Richardson & Barbara Maré. Cover design: Lynn Peck, Central Media.

National Library of New Zealand Cataloguing-in-Publication Data
Doherty, Joanne, 1952-
Mind Y'self Now, Jewarne : a Kiwi in Donegal & Dublin / Joanne Doherty.
ISBN 978-1-877448-35-5
1. Doherty, Joanne, 1952---Travel. 2. Ireland—Description and travel.
3. Ireland—Genealogy. 4. New Zealand—Genealogy. I. Title.
914.704824—dc 22

STEELE ROBERTS PUBLISHERS
Box 9321, Wellington, Aotearoa New Zealand
info@SteeleRoberts.co.nz • www.SteeleRoberts.co.nz

Contents

Foreword *7*

Acknowledgements *10*

1 Haere Ra and *Céad Míle Fáilte 11*

2 Exploring Letterkenny and Donegal *17*

3 Doon Rock and Sir Cahir O'Doherty *23*

4 Assumption Day and Ainslie *27*

5 Gartan and Glencolumbcille *36*

6 Belfast and Kilmacrennan *43*

7 Tory Island *48*

8 Ardoyne and Bloody Sunday *55*

9 A new job and 9/11 *61*

10 Farewell to Alice and Donegal *67*

11 Dublin views *74*

12 Remembering history *85*

13 Buses, language and gigs *92*

14 All Blacks and Van the Man *99*

15 *Lord of the Rings*, Christmas and the Pogues *107*

16 A new year dawns *114*

17 Waitangi Day and Ash Wednesday *122*

18 A Doherty pilgrimage and St Patrick's Day *129*

19 Easter in Scotland *137*

20 Italy and Pip *144*

21 *Olé! Olé! Olé! 154*

22 Patsy O'Reilly explores Ireland *163*

23 *Sláinte! Go raimh maith agat* (Cheers! Thank you) *173*

Epilogue *182*

Glossary *185*

Index *187*

FOREWORD

This book is an entrancing memoir of a year spent in Ireland by an extraordinary couple, Joanne and Jack Doherty. Joanne and Jack are from New Zealand, both have Irish ancestors, some of whom left Ireland during and after the Great Famine of the 1840s. Their year was to give them time to thoroughly explore what Joanne calls their second homeland. How and why they decided to live in Ireland is just one of the intriguing stories in this book.

Their first home in Ireland was close to their Kelly relatives in Letterkenny, County Donegal. Joanne's interest in people and her strong sense of family, present and past, permeate this book. She and Jack welcomed a stream of relatives and friends to Letterkenny and with them explored the ancient sites and beauty spots of Donegal. Joanne was as fascinated by the Irish myths and legends as she is with Maori legends and history of her native land. She makes many links between the old world and the new. For example, she describes the tapestries made by the women of Letterkenny that hang in the Heritage Centre on the shores of Lough Gartan. These tapestries tell the story of the Glenveigh evictions of 1861: "the landlord, John Adair, owned the site and closed the school with 30 children on the roll, ordering the soldiers to ram the houses. The people had to leave the district. Many families left for Perth in Western Australia, their names embroidered on the last tapestry were all familiar: Rodden my great-grandfather's name, Curran, Conaghan and Friel". These too were family names. One feels close to the Irish diaspora when reading this book.

With their money running out, Joanne and Jack moved to Dublin in search of jobs. Joanne was appointed chief officer to the Council for Children's Hospitals' Care in Ireland in 2001, where we worked together. Our task was to facilitate the three children's hospitals in Dublin to work together and leave behind their past rivalry. Joanne's gifts of wisdom and wit, her powers of observation and sensitivity towards people and situations, as well as her sense of humour, greatly contributed to the work of the Council, and likewise make this an engrossing book, although I am glad I did not know she was writing it at that time!

Jack was employed by the Eastern Regional Health Authority. They found a tiny apartment in the centre of the city, across the river from Temple Bar. This is how the first chapter on their life in Dublin opens: "Dublin is magic. After eight weeks in Donegal, I am ready for the buzz and bustle this city offers. Even Jack is adjusting quickly! Our Shoebox is warm and comfortable and answers all our needs. On our first day the sun bathed the rooms all afternoon and the moon shone on the Liffey river at night."

Soon the 'Shoebox' was bursting at the seams with the next raft of visitors, first of all their grown-up children came in relays, then cousins and friends from New Zealand — all to be shown the sights of Dublin and its hinterland. The passage grave at Newgrange, Co. Meath was a special favourite to which visitors from New Zealand were brought, and rightly so, as it is a wonder of the Celtic world.

Dublin comes alive in the book as Joanne and Jack explore it with friends and family. There is the buzz of the city itself, its libraries and art galleries; the beauty and calm of a walk through Trinity College and onto Stephen's Green; the buskers on Grafton Street; the political marches and commemorations; the concerts and singing pubs; the rugby and soccer matches watched in a warm and friendly pub. Dublin Tourism could adopt this book!

But Joanne is aware of the darker side of the city too. Kilmainham Jail both fascinated and depressed her. The awfulness of the Irish immigration system which she experienced while applying for a work visa. It was not herself she was worried about but the new immigrants from Africa and Asia, often with small children, with little knowledge of English and no interpreter, having to wait for hours and an uncertain outcome at the end. There were also the homeless and the beggars on the streets and some too proud to beg but desperate nevertheless. "The old man at the bus stop outside Trinity College stands in his long brown raincoat waiting for people to catch the bus and throw their cigarette butts away. He quickly stoops to collect them and puts them in his pocket."

This book is about more than Donegal and Dublin. There are vignettes too from their many travels around the country and to Northern Ireland, as well as their visits to Scotland, Wales and Tuscany. There are lovely poems too written by Joanne and Jack.

I have kept the Doherty's genuine interest in Northern Ireland, its people and politics, until last. They still have relatives living in the North, whom they visited on several occasions. Jack had met Paddy Doherty, that outstanding community worker and leader in Derry city, on an earlier visit to the North. He was part of what led them to spend real time on this island, as the book relates.

Joanne describes being nervous about visiting the North during her first week or so in Donegal as she remembered it as rather frightening on an earlier visit. Letterkenny is close to Derry — a city they love — but in a very short time she found that she now thought nothing of crossing the border.

Joanne and Jack, like so many of us, wished passionately for peace and justice in Northern Ireland. While reading Joanne's manuscript over the last few days in preparation for writing this foreword, I found myself wishing so much that she and Jack were here to be part of the momentous events taking place in Ireland during this first week in May 2007, as the peace process at last comes to fruition. To have seen Ian Paisley, the loyalist leader and Martin McGuinness of Sinn Féin, installed in Stormont as First Minister and Deputy First Minister, smiling at each other, was almost unbelievable after all those years of conflict. One senses a genuine spirit of goodwill across the different leaders and communities, north and south, to go on working together to generate tolerance, respect and justice on this island. Oh, how much Joanne and Jack would have loved to have been part of this incredible week, but they are with us in spirit anyway.

Helen Burke PhD
West Cork, Ireland
May 2007

Dr Helen Burke is emeritus professor, University College Dublin, National University of Ireland, and the co-author of the authorised biography of Mary Robinson.

Joanne and Helen.

ACKNOWLEDGEMENTS

Many achievements in my life have involved a community effort, and writing this book has been no different. When I arrived home from Ireland my friend John Faisandier presented me with a book of the emails I had written saying, "You have to publish these." Several others agreed, including strangers who approach me even now saying "Are you the woman who wrote those emails from Ireland? You should publish them!"

When Frances Cherry, the New Zealand author, advertised her *Write That Book* course in my community newspaper, I stood in the kitchen and said out loud to myself "Yes — I will." My homework every month was to write one or two chapters and Frances and my fellow students provided an encouraging space with good ideas, comments and feedback. The book slowly but surely grew to completion.

In Easter 2006 the manuscript was blessed in a cabin at Waiohine in the South Wairarapa. The book and I were ready to part. My niece, Emma Hayes, found Myra Mortlock to review the manuscript: she is Jewish but has never lived in her homeland and could identify closely with the influences of culture, religion and family that Irish and Jewish people experience. After returning the manuscript, we shared an Irish whiskey and Myra talked of her new decision to visit Ireland!

John and Josie MacInnes, Jack's twin sister and her husband, generously printed copies of the manuscript, reproducing the photographs to a much better quality and sharing their expertise and advice on layout and content.

Sending it to publishers was the next step. When I sent my five children to primary school, I hoped the world would understand and appreciate them as well as I did and patted myself on the back for a reasonable, if not perfect, effort. This was similar. I had loved living the story, and writing about it gave me time to savour on every page that Irish experience of the people and their craic, the music and history of their land and its physical beauty, including the weather!

So many friends and family have supported me in writing this book. Two women anchored me on either side of the world with their wisdom and aroha — Teresea Olsen in Aotearoa New Zealand and Helen Burke in Ireland. Roze Doherty and Stephen King shared their talents as artists and photographers with ideas for the cover and the maps, and Pip Desmond and I enjoyed encouraging each other to complete the writing of our books.

Most of all I want to thank Jack, a quintessential Irish Kiwi, and everyone else who believes in me and provides their love and support for me as a writer, but more importantly as a woman, a mother, a granny GoJo, a sister and a friend.

This book is for you, first of all.

Haere Ra and Céad Míle Fáilte

We are on our way to live in Ireland. It is July 2001 and today, across the road in Sunshine Bay, our friend Huia is filming, making a documentary about Jack's journey to Ireland. The process began early this morning with a mihi and karakia, a Maori greeting and prayer. I am watching from the deck above the water. My story about being in Ireland is part of Jack's story and both are about to begin.

This journey is more tangible this morning and I am left wondering why the adventure feels exciting, curious and insecure all at the same time. When I ponder why we are doing this, a few strands emerge. First because I want to, then because I love Jack and he needs to do this. But, finally, I know it is also about the generations before me and those that will follow. This makes the journey ahead very small, because it is only a tiny part of what started a long time ago, and very big because of its role in our future.

The journey is also a tribute to Myles, Bridget, Bernard, Elizabeth, Catherine, John, Mary and John, our grandparents and great-grandparents who left Ireland to come to Aotearoa New Zealand. We will connect with our family names of Doherty, McPadden, Rodden, McGuinness, Phelan, Kirwan, Clune, Caddigan and Byrne as we go to their counties of Leitrim, Clare, Fermanagh, Donegal, Derry and Waterford to experience 'home', and to be at home, in Ireland.

Yesterday was filled with rich hours to savour. In the middle of a wild storm we packed up the house and stored furniture in the garage and basement. Several treasures were packed away in my heart at the same time. We laughed and enjoyed the time with our children, Josh and his wife Roze, Hannah and her husband Michael, Alice (who is travelling with us) and our niece Emma. Emma's backpack has been overseas several times and she insisted it needed another outing with us — to Ireland! Our friends Mars and Helen arrived with their friend (another Alice) who is from Carrickmacross in County Monaghan, carrying a basket of hot scones for afternoon tea and a delicious chicken and mushroom filo for dinner. Our every need was answered.

Any sense of grief I have is focused on Hannah, more than any of my children. I will also miss the spring smell of freesias that my friend Nuala and I enjoy so much. Just in case there are none in Ireland, I found some at the market this morning to have on the kitchen table until we leave.

A week to go and we are sweeping paths, picking up the cabbage tree leaves that are perpetually falling, and clearing the section after the storm. The harbour is flat and milky today and the sun bright. My sister Kate came early in the day to say goodbye and made me pause for lunch. I showed her how in sync I was with the shags on the rocks after the storm — they were standing on the rocks holding their wings out to dry while I was hanging out our sheets and towels.

Today my list is long. I am wrapping up music tapes and aromatherapy 'sleep ease' for my sister Maree ('Ma') to use in her new job, disbelieving that I will miss her whole year in Wellington after forever wanting her to live closer. I have identified the website to buy the tickets for the All Black test in Ireland, rushed in to sign the documents for the new Waiohine property that we now own with our friend Pip, tracked down my daughter Jessica's tax refund to send to her in Sydney, and made a smoked fish pie for the plasterers who are finishing our bedroom.

Alice held a farewell party last night for her friends amid the boxes and piles of belongings that are now appearing all over the house. We had a McPadden and Doherty farewell last week. When three-year-old Millie Tui danced an Irish jig at the party, I cried. Our friends Katie and Jules hosted a dinner, which was also very special. Three-year-old Moana patted my back and told me my "big brother Alice" was crying when Mars sang 'Raglan Road' for us. What a close network to say goodbye to, and what an adventure to dream of having.

It started five years earlier, when Jack was diagnosed with cancer. As we all recovered from the shock, and later the harrowing treatment, it became a time for Jack and me to reflect on how and where we were living our lives. We identified changes we wanted to make in case our time together was to be limited. Our first decision was to live by the sea, and by the end of that year we were living on Wellington harbour. Our home at Sunshine Bay has a 180° view across to Wellington city and out towards Cook Strait and the South Island. The house is ten metres from the sea and surrounded by native trees. The Irish flag flies on the flagpole at the front gate.

The more audacious goal of going to live in Ireland for a year or two began to take shape. We had holidayed in Ireland before, but after we had become used to city life in Wellington, this more serious dream of Jack's emerged and gained momentum. Our five children seemed settled. We had celebrated Hannah and Michael's, then Josh and Roze's, spring weddings the year before. Jude was flatting and working as a *barista* in between surfing and snowboarding seasons, and Jessica (Jec) was in Sydney. Alice would come with us and spend her last year of secondary schooling in Donegal.

My life with Jack has had an adventurous side to it since we met and married. We belong to Te Wakaiti, a community we created as hippies and self-appointed reformers of the Catholic Church. We set up a trust to buy land near Featherston in the Wairarapa. This environment and our commitment to it has enriched our lives with vision, fun and challenge. It has encouraged us to trust, to think differently and to grow. Going to Ireland was to be the next adventure to unfold.

The day we leave New Zealand our tenants arrive early to collect the keys and discuss last-minute details. They have recently arrived from inland India and are excited about living by the sea. A vase of early daffodils sits on the table to welcome them. In return they give us half of an azure crystal to take to Ireland, saying it reminds them of the view from our windows. They will keep the other half so we will know our home is treasured and looked after. Every moment before we leave Aotearoa feels emotionally charged. This unexpected exchange with the tenants we have only just met is part of that.

We cry as we say goodbye to our children, sisters and brothers and friends at the airport. Many college students are there to farewell Alice. In the middle of them all is Father Barney Doherty, Jack's cousin, with the widest beaming smile and waving arms. He has arrived at the airport on foot, grey and breathless, announcing that someone from the Doherty family needs to be there. I send some of Alice's friends off to find a wheelchair for him. As we wait, he calls me aside and says quietly, "I really want to thank you for loving Kev [Jack] the way you do." I am taken aback at this intimate farewell from Jack's much-loved older cousin.

On the plane, I am bereft — overwhelmed at the depth of our feelings for the family and friends we have just farewelled. I wonder at the experiences ahead and how changed we, and they, will be by the time we return.

Thirty hours later we are about to catch our first glimpse of Ireland. The Irish Sea looks grey but the excitement and expectation are mounting. We crane our necks to see the first green field through the drizzling rain. Suddenly, there it is — row upon row of brown and white houses spreading out from Dublin and treading on the low green hills that surround this burgeoning city. I am crying at the sight of a homeland I have never lived in, then I want to leap and dance off the plane.

Jack walks triumphantly through the EEC line at Customs, clutching tightly the Irish passport that was a 50th birthday present to himself. Alice and I wait to receive a three-month stamp in our passports, with advice to report to the nearest police station to have the time extended. We walk over a doormat on our entry into Ireland. It is the Irish answer to the recent foot-and-mouth disease outbreak, and it looks just like the mat at the back door at home.

We walk into the welcoming smile of Emmett Devlin, our Kiwi friend who shifted to Dublin a year ago. It is surprising to all be here in Dublin; our last time together was at Hiruharama on the Whanganui River, where we discussed the pros and cons of living in Ireland. Now here we are, living the dream. We drive to Emmett, Tricia, Joseph and Siobhan's house for a meal welcoming us and farewelling their friend Jo, who is flying home to New Zealand the next day.

The Devlin home is an unofficial New Zealand embassy with many Kiwis enjoying their hospitality and company when they land in Dublin. (In the same way, my great-grandfather Myles McPadden provided hospitality and accommodation in Westport, New Zealand, to immigrants from Ireland, including 16-year-old Bridget Clune, a dairymaid from Quin in County Clare, whom he later married.)

Next morning we board the double-decker into the city. The side of the bus is covered with advertising for a Mary Black concert. Footpaths and bridges are crowded. Moving around is difficult and I am constantly distracted by Dublin's smells, buildings and people. All day Alice and I point out familiar-looking faces. "Look", I say, "that girl is so like Sophie Wooles," and Alice replies, "I've been seeing her all day today — she's so Irish!" Sometimes we nudge each other, laughing, unable to even say the name, as a replica of an aunty or cousin or friend walks past. Everyone looks familiar. Grafton Street has the expected press of shoppers, tourists, flower sellers and buskers, all competing for space on the pavement, and I hope I will be able to spend days absorbing Dublin.

In the afternoon it rains heavily. The cobblestones are black and slippery; car tyres sound like whips cracked against a wall. We walk across O'Connell Bridge, through the maze of bars, cafés and shops that is Temple Bar and back across the Ha'penny Bridge. Dublin is lively and busy as we dodge the people walking, biking, singing and begging, and those just standing still, like me, taking it all in.

We return 'home' for dinner laden with produce from the Devlins' local supermarket, including South African mandarins, French cheese, Italian wine and Irish soda bread. Emmett gives us a quick introduction to Gaelic football and the teams in the semifinals at the weekend, including his favourite, Tyrone. He proudly shows off his collection of red and white Tyrone flags and buntings, which he displays outside the house at the weekend. They are carefully stored with his All Black flags.

When we phone Jack's cousins the Kellys, in Donegal, they announce that our house is all furnished and ready. We head north in our rental car, stopping in Carrickmacross for lunch. In this delightful town the rows of red, blue, yellow and white shops are decorated with hanging baskets of flowers. Later in the afternoon we arrive in Letterkenny, a four-hour drive from Dublin.

"*Céad míle fáilte*", says Tommy Kelly in his soft voice as he opens the front door. In the cosy lounge he claps his hands together, smiling and saying, "Well! Well!

Céad míle fáilte," over and over. The warmth and hospitality of Tommy, Margaret and their family feels exactly like the hundred thousand welcomes of the greeting. Margaret and her daughter Irene are busy finding out about our family and trying to comprehend why anyone would ever want to come and live in Donegal, away from our South Pacific paradise. Our photos of snow-covered mountains cannot persuade them that New Zealanders do not lie under palm trees on white sandy beaches all day. We follow them in the car to see our new home in Clachan Mor. It belongs to their sons John and Kevin, and is just two doors away from their daughter Irene's home.

Clachan Mor is at the top of the Letterkenny hill, above the hospital. It is a cul-de-sac of semi-detached houses that all look the same. The house numbers run 1, 3, 4, 5, 6 then 14, so we drive past our number 14 on the first attempt, then several more times! No distinguishing feature marks it as our house, unlike at home where we might see the blue roof or the trellis gate. The cosy two-storey home will be a new way of living for us. The rooms are small with no open-plan living or French doors leading onto spacious decks. The kitchen and dining area is generous with a smaller lounge and three bedrooms upstairs. All the windows are double-glazed and an oil supply at the back door heats the house and hot water. And living next door, it turns out, is another Mrs Doherty.

It is a week later and I spot the full moon across the Donegal hills. The sky is pink, the street quiet at six o'clock on a midsummer morning. The steeple of St Eunan's cathedral watches over Letterkenny and the rows and rows of houses are tied like ribbon across the low hills. The street we live in is quiet all day. In the early evening dozens of children appear to play hide-and-seek and ride

Hey You Guys!

Whilst settling in once tears are over
Remember you're an Irish rover
You'll come of age and find the saviour
Travelling causes strange behaviour

Slowing down, you'll look around
The people, land will all astound
Reflected mirrors on cultural walls
Cascade away like waterfalls

This life is worth as much as *all*
Shall roll again a perfect ball
Have you landed yet?
I bet

Your experiences gallant or grave
Will always mystically amaze
And in yourself you've always known
That we are waiting "the same, at *home*"

So stay and play the Irish way
The way you want to play today
You are more than okay
Living the Irish day

Jude Doherty

their bikes until dark. Several times boys have knocked on our front door giggling, asking if we want to buy potatoes. I am as attracted to their strange accent as they are to mine.

I notice we are the only ones in the street who have the windows open. Mrs Doherty next door has commented on this, and the Irish cousins are highly amused at our Kiwi flip-flops and bare feet. A few weeks later when I walk to the Kelly house in shoes and socks, they say, "I see you're dressing Irish now."

Mrs Doherty moved to Letterkenny from Kilmacrennan, five miles away, where she lived next door to Kitty Rodden. My great-grandparents were Roddens from Kilmacrennan, so it is hard not to sense connection. The headstone of my great-grandmother, Catherine Byrne, in the Lyell cemetery on the West Coast of the South Island bears the words "native of Donegal". Living in this part of Ireland it feels like we are in the right place to begin this adventure. Letterkenny is bigger than I imagined, with the rows of houses gathered in pockets known as estates. It's like we are all living in barracks. Because we are near the top of the hill and in the last line of houses there is a country lane behind our house that Alice and I enjoy walking or running along.

It has been a difficult and emotional week. We wonder why we are here and think often of those we have left behind. Alice and I have cried a lot, and Jack certainly looks as if he needs to. This will be a strange year ahead, picking blackberries in September and daffodils in February.

Helen O'Connell has sent a timely email reminding us how many of our friends and family want to be where we are right now. My heart nudges forward. Then Jude sends a poem responding to our homesickness that makes me stop and smile and again enjoy being in Ireland.

Doherty Keep, Buncrana.

2

Exploring Letterkenny and Donegal

The beauty of this north-west corner called Donegal exemplifies the physical beauty of Ireland that we recall from songs, poetry and stories told by our grandmothers. The wild coast of Glencolumbcille, the summer festival in Rathmullen, the fishing village of Killybegs, and Donegal castle and town are early gems we discover. This corner of Ireland in and around Lough Swilly has rolling, gentle, low hills cut into squares of every shade of green. The housing has increased everywhere since our last visit almost ten years ago, and throughout Donegal, two-storey homes have replaced many of the thatched cottages.

In Glenties, a town in Donegal we find our niece, Liz Doherty, sitting on the footpath reading in the sun. Alice and I are excited that someone so familiar is coming to stay. Liz spends her time looking after us, cooking us meals and handing out vitamin B and evening primrose tablets for stress. She encourages us to be pragmatic, while giving us warm hugs to help us overcome our apprehension and uncertainty. A few days later, Sarah, who has grown up with our children, steps off the bus from Dublin calling, "Welcome Dohertys to Ireland," and waving a bottle of Baileys in the air. Both she and Liz look after us well — a role reversal after our years of loving and nurturing them both as children.

Together we visit the ancient ring fort Grianán of Aileach that overlooks Lough Swilly and Inch Island. Beyond the Grianán a 360° panorama takes in the Swilly, the Inishowen Peninsula, Loch Foyle and the city of Derry. The Grianán was the home of the descendants of Niall of the Nine Hostages, High King of Ireland in the fourth century AD. From the top of the five-metre stone walls there is a strategic

The ancient ring fort, Grianán of Aileach.

view over seven counties. Behind the gently curved exterior of the ring fort is a fernery in the bog, where it is said that St Patrick baptised the sons of Niall. The Doherty clan claims ancestry from one of those sons.

The ancient architecture of the Grianán is replicated in the modern Catholic church at the base of the hill, and a stone mural at the entrance to the church tells the history of the stronghold. Local stories say an underground passage connects the Grianán to nearby Burt Castle, and hidden in the hills of the Grianán lie a thousand sleeping warriors, who with their horses will rise up one day to reclaim what they have lost.

Wolfe Tone, one of the leaders of the 1789 rebellion against English rule, was arrested near the Doherty Keep in Buncrana. From here are gentle walks down to the sea or along the river bed under the oak trees. Directly across the Swilly from Buncrana is Ramelton, from where the Gaelic chiefs fled during the flight of the earls.

We travel to the Doherty Keep along Sir Cahir O'Doherty Avenue. Sir Cahir, the last Gaelic chief, befriended the English and was knighted by them. But when they began to take the land of Inishowen, part of the plantations of Ulster, he rose up against them and was assassinated at Doon Rock on 18 July 1608.

We return home via Derry, the city of the Dohertys, where Alice helps me with my first visit to an internet café. They offer a special deal on latte and cake with thirty minutes online. This is a mistake. I am busy learning to navigate a new keyboard and screen view. Time flies, and my coffee is cold!

Oscaill Chathaoir Uí Dhochartaigh
CAHIR O'DOHERTY AVENUE

It is raining here today, as it does most days even if only for a while. When I go for milk and bread the woman at the shop remarks, "It's a grey day, but close, mind." I have noticed that 'close' is used to describe any temperature over 15°. Another day I meet a woman in a shop doorway. It is sunny, and when I comment on the day she replies, "Ooh now dear, it's fair droughty, y'know. Jesus, Mary and Joseph, there's been no rain at all this week." The weather is a favourite topic of conversation. The Irish apologise constantly to us for the "desprit weather we're givin' you." We, in return, assure them we haven't come for the weather.

In between our tourist days we visit the employment centre, talk to a personnel consultant, look into cheap options for buying a car (to discover there are none, because of insurance costs) and manage, at last, to connect the phone and internet at home. We receive our first mail in the letterbox, a card showing a dresser of blue and white china from our niece Sarah Doherty "in case you are missing yours from home," she writes, and a card with harakeke weaving — New Zealand flax — from our friend Pip. It's as if we have won a treasure chest, with mail in the letterbox and access to email from the kitchen table.

The length of our stay here in Ireland depends on finding work. Our New Zealand dollars are rapidly disappearing. It is different from when we have holidayed here before. Do we just have another holiday and return home, given that jobs and income are not coming quickly enough? Or do we get into debt, waiting to find work?

Donegal is one of the Gaelic-speaking areas of Ireland known as the Gaeltacht. For many of the health and education jobs we both could apply for Irish is a prerequisite. My own Irish language is limited to *feck* and I don't think my pronunciation of even this is always correct. Instead, we have applied for a varied and amusing range of jobs in or near Letterkenny, including hardware shop assistant, garden centre labourer, hotel receptionist and accounts manager. (From some we will still be awaiting for a response three years later.)

I always read the local newspaper whenever I am away from home and Ireland has numerous small, medium and large ones. Letterkenny has a range, as does the whole of County Donegal. The articles in the national newspapers are more informative and provocative than those in New Zealand.

The media, and society in general, while still permeated with things Catholic, are also surprisingly secular. In last week's local paper the parish priest in Buncrana was 'giving out' about chewing gum being stuck under the church pews. He has been asking people to remove it before he gives them Holy Communion, and he says he will now have to make a regular double announcement

The external wall of the Grianán.

before Mass about removing chewing gum and turning off mobile phones that interrupt the service.

The public service broadcaster in Ireland is known as RTE, Radio Telefís Éireann, and the television news is on RTE each night at 6.01. It is preceded by the Angelus for one minute, and while the Angelus bells ring the screen shows people in various situations pausing to pray. Alice has discovered that *Shortland Street*, the New Zealand soap opera, is on Irish television at 2.30 in the morning.

The advertisements in the media here are amusing. The Inland Revenue Department is reminding people to pay their tax on time and Mrs Doyle, the long-suffering housekeeper from the television series *Father Ted*, is on the screen urging viewers to pay their tax on time, with the words "Go on, go on, go on," in the same insistent way she offers her sandwiches to the reluctant priests in the presbytery. A mobile phone company advertising on bus shelters warns "no text on the first date" and later in Dublin we see a billboard for a new gay magazine showing two male Gaelic footballers embracing and kissing. The words underneath the photograph read "Relax! It's a gay thing!" Ireland feels more liberal than when I was first here.

Alice and I explore Letterkenny and visit the school she will go to when the summer holidays end in six weeks. It looks bleak and uninviting and quite unlike St Eunan's, the grand school for boys up the road. We look at the school magazine and although Irish school life will be quite a change, the names of the girls are familiar — Dohertys, Maguires, McCaffertys, McFaddens, O'Reillys and Kellys.

Cottage in County Donegal.

The main street of Letterkenny is narrow and steep with shops crammed in beside pubs, lawyers' offices, banks and newsagents. We arrive at nine to photocopy CVs at the library and continue the arduous process of opening a bank account. However, the library doesn't open until midday, the bank at ten and the internet cafés at eleven. Realising we need to adjust to this slower pace of life, we head for the shops.

At a glance, the shops remind me of New Plymouth's main street in the 1960s when I was growing up. If the Warehouse superstore ever comes to Ireland, small shops like these will disappear and the unemployment rate will soar. In the draper's shop a staff of five walk around the uneven slope of the wooden floor. I instantly recognise a unique smell from my childhood. The shelves are stocked with brown cardboard boxes labelled in capital letters SOCKS Size 8; NYLONS 98 p; SINGLETS, boys; and FIRST COMMUNION RIBBON. Mrs Duffy, as her badge announces, serves us at the counter. Over her right shoulder I see a coloured photo of John F Kennedy. We ask about the girls' school uniform and Alice's interest wanes even more when Mrs Duffy replies, "Dark brown skirt, dark brown jersey, dark brown socks and of course dark brown shoes, worn with a lemon shirt." Mrs Duffy walks us to the door, her hands in her faded apron pockets. She looks up at the overcast sky and says, "It's a grey day. You'll be alright if the rain keeps up."

The shop next door sells summer tops and skirts, and when Alice takes a T-shirt to the counter the young woman moves her ashtray to swipe the credit card. In another shop, the girl and the man who work there are eating fish and chips at the counter. Shopping in Letterkenny is a culture shock.

The Letterkenny library is a great source of both fiction and non-fiction books. I find Patricia Grace's *Cousins* there. Last weekend the *Irish Times* had a full-page article about this Maori writer. I get lost for hours in the bookshops here.

New Zealand has historic rugby links in Donegal as the very first captain of the All Blacks was a Donegal man, Dave Gallaher, from Ramelton. He emigrated to New Zealand when he was six and died on the battlefields of France in the First World War. The Letterkenny rugby club has since renamed its home ground the Dave Gallaher Memorial Ground and adopted a new crest with the silver fern, and a new black strip.

Our Kelly cousins, Margaret and Tommy are in their 80s and visit us often to make sure we are feeling at home. Margaret always has a bar of chocolate in her bag for Alice, and she and Tommy are forever keen to hear of our latest explorations of Donegal. They are astonished at the ground we have covered so far. Margaret responds to all our stories with exclamations of "Jesus, Mary and Blessed St Joseph" or, on one occasion, "Oh Sacred Heart of Divinity!" It is worth keeping her talking just to hear the invocations that ripple across the conversation. I am becoming more familiar with the language of my great-grandmothers.

Sir Cahir Rua

Standing on O'Donnell's Rock of Doon
I hear lead penetrate your red-headed skull.
I flinch.
I too look towards the Swilly
Alas, our Earls had flown, Ulster defeated.

Alone you fought the last battle
for the High Kings of Ireland
Royal crowns were changing
England's crown to reign.

From your past to my future
It will never be the same.

Your castles of Inch and Carrickbraghy taken
Now for me, ruins.
Culmore laid waste. Derry torched.
Inishowen fallen.

Elizabeth knighted you once
Now you turn to slay her successor
She took it all, Chichester's gain
You were left with only the struggle.

The redcoat's aim was true
Your blood spilled on Doon
Your O'Dogherty troops castrated and banished
Your body drawn and quartered in Derry.

"Let no one do this again," they decreed
As they thrust your bearded head on a pole
And displayed you at the gates of Dublin Castle.
The English Crown's warning.

Four centuries later I stand at these castle gates
To remember you and enjoy your free city
I salute you, my cousin,
For your daring, for your stand.

Jack Doherty

Colmcille's Abbey, Gartan.

3

Doon Rock and Sir Cahir O'Doherty

St Colmcille's birthplace is in Gartan in County Donegal. In the stone ruins of the Colmcille abbey is a grotto where mementos have been left. They include pieces of material and rosary beads, but also toys, pictures, ribbons, asthma inhalers, bus tickets, hair combs, aspirin packets and babies' dummies.

In the graveyard we see the names of many of our own families and friends from home — Dohertys, Conaghans, O'Reillys and McCaffertys — and a headstone engraved with the red hand of Ulster.

Near Glen Veagh National Park and in the middle of a moor, our little rental car gets firmly stuck in the bog. Alice films the great escape while Jack, our friend Sarah and I literally lift the car up and out of the bog and back on to the road. On our return to Letterkenny we call in at Doon Rock and Doon Well, a sacred place known for the crowning of the O'Donnell chieftains and where Sir Cahir O'Doherty was shot by the British. They took his body to Derry but his head to Dublin to deter anyone considering fighting for indigenous land rights. It is hardly surprising that with our Irish heritage we understand and support the rights of the indigenous Maori to their land in New Zealand.

Remembrance plaque, Buncrana Bridge.

"O'Dochartaigh"
Chief of Inishowen
In memory of a leader and warrior
Cahir 'Rua' O'Dogherty
The last chieftain of an ancient Gaelic civilization
1587–1608
killed by the oppressive British forces at Doon Rock,
Kilmacrennan 18th July 1608

At Doon Rock we take a short walk through the pink heather to the hidden Mass rock, where Catholics would gather in secret to pray and celebrate their forbidden Mass.

At the Doon well you kneel to collect holy water. A plaque explains that to give your special request or 'intention' the best chance to be answered, you must recite the Hail Mary, Our Father and the long Apostles' Creed five times. The last sentence on the plaque reads "All prayers must be recited in bare feet". It is pouring with rain and icy cold the day we visit. The tree beside the holy well drips with mementos like those in the abbey. Dozens of multi-coloured rosary beads dangle in the rain on the branches beside pieces of coloured material and other memorabilia like film canisters, personal letters and more asthma inhalers. Visitors from Ulster begin their prayers and walk the circuit around the well, removing their shoes and socks to reveal the whitest feet I have ever seen.

Today's news is that the Northern Ireland Parliament has been suspended for twenty-four hours, followed by the IRA's statement that they are withdrawing their offer to decommission their arms. It is like observing a giant game of chess, the rules of which I do not know or understand. The Good Friday agreement now requires both sides to show good faith for it to continue. The IRA say there is not enough commitment from the Loyalists to warrant a substantial move to decommission, so when Parliament is suspended again they express their disapproval in this way.

The newspapers carry numerous political commentaries and I am enjoying having the time to read them all and to think and write — one of the advantages of unemployment.

Death and memorial notices in the newspapers often have a black cross above them, and mention 'the remains' arriving at the church at 10 a.m. for the rosary or Requiem Mass, or being taken home for the wake. Living near Letterkenny Hospital, we notice long lines of cars and people gathering before going back to the house where the body will be 'waked' until going to the church for the Requiem Mass. Our Irish cousins explain how they waked Aunty Mary back at their home. The body is accompanied at all times. Businesses are often closed if a friend or relative of an employer has died. A sign is left in the window or doorway: "Out of respect for … this shop will be closed over the time of the funeral."

Months later, driving in the west of Ireland with our children Jec, Josh and Roze, we hear a long litany on Galway radio of the names of those who have died in the past week, and the village or town in which they lived. Cremations are relatively new here, but are becoming more frequent as family die in England or abroad and their ashes come home to be buried. Death in Ireland has its own rituals and meanings, but I have no difficulty in relating these to my own experience of burying my parents, and the Maori tangi or funeral rituals.

Talkback radio is a constant source of entertainment as we travel around Donegal. Today callers are phoning about warts. An 80-year-old man has rung to say that when he had over seventy warts on his hands he decided to visit the well-known grave of the 'jealous man and woman' in Galway. He rubbed a sewing pin on the warts and left it on the grave. Later, when the pin began to rust, the warts fell off. He assured the listeners that the grave was covered in rusty pins. Once before he had seen a doctor who had burnt the warts off, leaving ugly scars. But with the pin, he exclaimed, "You won't believe it — dere's no scarring at all, at all."

The next caller alleges his warts finally disappeared after he shook hands in Grafton Street with Bono, the lead singer of U2. An older woman follows, explaining how she shook hands with the rock star just after the previous caller and, for the first time in her life, her hands became covered in warts. The calls about warts continue for an hour, and we hear several follow-up calls over the next week.

Many callers also offer their condolences to Bono, whose father is critically ill. He passes away a week later. U2 are ending their world tour at this time, with over 160,000 at the two concerts at Slane Castle. The Garda comment in the local newspapers that the concert has gone well, with no one at all attempting to swim the Boyne River this year. The concert includes a special tribute from Bono to his dad. In an interview he talks of his mum dying suddenly when he was 14, leaving his dad to raise him and his brother. The boys often had to ask their dad to turn the music down. The father had a fine tenor voice and told Bono that it was a shame he didn't have a voice like his father's, as he could have done something with it!

Exam results have arrived in the mail, so talkback callers are 'giving out' about the Leaving Certificate results causing drunkenness in the young. They blame the laddish culture for girls doing better than boys. The whole country is talking constantly about preparing for the Leaving Certificate, or awaiting the Leaving Certificate results, or working out the implications of tertiary study once the results are known. For three days, every conversation I hear in the supermarket, the post office or on the footpaths of Letterkenny is about the Leaving Certificate results.

Many callers are upset about the possibility of smoke-free bars being introduced into Ireland. A publican phones, adamant that cigarette smoke contributes greatly to the atmosphere in Irish bars. Smokers are even haranguing the Minister of Health for forcing them to catch pneumonia by smoking outside. Topical health issues here are similar to those in New Zealand — smoking, head lice, campylobacter, saying no to power pylons, and a growing two-tier health system where your income and private medical insurance determine your access to health services.

The newspapers report that Tony Blair is flying his family economy class with Ryanair on their holiday; he is determined to use an Irish airline this time. Choosing Ryanair is creating a furore with the trade unions, and the Irish are quick to rename the airline Ryan Blair as a temporary marketing strategy. Irish humour is woven through every facet of life, and I love it.

Being in Ireland

for Jack

I muse about the deeper purpose
Of this time in Ireland
Homeland

I know what it means
But I wonder about the timing
In our life of loving and living

This time in Ireland
Homeland
Is a gift of time — from me

Your children gift it too
Watching you relish and embrace it
Like you do all of your time

What will our three decades grow to?
I will be satisfied fully
When it is complete
Soon or not

Burt Castle, County Donegal.

4

ASSUMPTION DAY AND AINSLIE

Today is 15 August, Assumption Day. The sun is shining brightly, with blue skies and a breeze, so the sheets and towels are on the clothesline. Jack and I go to the cathedral for midday Mass to remember his dad who passed away twenty-four years ago today. He had prayed the Rosary every evening for many years, so Assumption Day was a significant day for him to be welcomed home.

St Eunan's cathedral is impressive, with a steeple that we can see from our house. The bishop's imposing house is across the road from the cathedral, and next door is a straggle of caravans belonging to the travelling people. It is insensitive to refer to them as gypsies or tinkers. They are the 'travelling' community and we belong to the 'settled' community. The children from the travelling community play in the cathedral carpark, their horses eating any vegetation they can find, including the bishop's shrubs.

An article in the local paper is about one of the travelling women, a mother of eleven, who has been waiting for a council house for twenty-seven years. One evening, driving past the bishop's house, we see a man washing down his white horse with long caressing strokes, watched by two of the smaller children. I'm not sure if they and the bishop have dinner together occasionally, or whether the beggars on the path as I step out of the cathedral doors belong to this same community of caravan dwellers at the edge of the cathedral carpark.

The carpark area is crammed for this Mass. We double park and pop quickly into the cathedral to find it too is over-full, everyone waiting quietly for Mass to begin. We discuss the likelihood of a traffic fine on a Holy Day in Ireland and decide to take the risk. Eventually the priest arrives, with several altar boys and

27

two altar men. He is a young man and wears a black hat. He begins to say Mass with his back to us, reads the epistle in Latin, takes off and replaces his hat seven or eight times during the sung 'Gloria', then reads the gospel in Latin with his back to us. When he delivers his sermon he faces the congregation, talking about the rosary disappearing from the home with the inevitable result of marriages ending, and empty convents and seminaries.

We discuss the carpark situation again and remain on our pews. However after the sermon, when the priest reminds everyone that communion will only be served under the tongue, and only if kneeling at the altar rails, we decide a traffic fine is too risky and leave. I wonder if Dad Doherty would have stayed, or moved with the times like us. I suspect he would have stayed.

Malin Head is the northernmost tip of Ireland and after Buncrana the drive through the Gap of Mamore is a long, steep, lane leading to a breathtaking view over the mountain, and down another equally long, steep lane across a patchwork quilt of green fields to the coast. At the gap is the holy well of Mamore and a collection of shrines, including a tall shrine to Mary and Bernadette, and a middle-sized shrine for the Little King, the Infant of Prague.

Shrines at the Gap of Mamore.

My mother always had a statue of the Little King on the mantelpiece or at the front of the china cabinet, believing it would mean she would never be short of money. He may have nodded off from time to time when she was busy praying for his intercession.

At the well I am using the collection of mugs and cups to fill my bottle with holy water when Alice (reminding me of Goldilocks discovering the three chairs), shrieks, "Ooh, there's a tiny wee baby one over there!" In a grotto is a minute statue of Padre Pio, a popular saint of Irish Catholics.

The northern coastal hills of Donegal have thatched white cottages sprinkled amid the dramatic scenery. On our way to the famine village on Doagh Island we drive past a hall with a sign *Gaelic Tug of War Club* on its door. For a very reasonable fee we receive a cup of tea, a piece of Irish soda bread and a plain biscuit before "your man" provides a guided tour around the village. He explains the living conditions, the wakes, education under the hedges, and Masses being said in secret behind big rocks.

The Irish were banned from any agricultural activity that competed with the English, including sheep farming. The land at this northernmost tip of Ireland is not fertile like other parts of Donegal and during the famine the poor were made to work for their food. Today, there are miles of stone walls and roads going nowhere all over the Donegal hills. They look like raised grey threads on top of the patchwork of pale green hills. The guide makes the connection to today's world, where the developed countries starve the rest of the world by not sharing power and resources.

Not far from Malin Head we discover the A. Doherty pub and enjoy a drink with Anthony Doherty, the publican.

Around the Inishowen Peninsula, at each strategic point, are Doherty castle ruins. Closer to Letterkenny are Burt and Inch Castles. We explore them all and are particularly drawn to the ruins at Carrickbraghy Castle towards the north of Inishowen.

The straight-edged walls that remain hint of the architecture and strength of this strategic castle on the northern point of Doagh Isle. Local records say it dates back to 811. It was from here in 1608 that Sir Cahir O'Doherty planned his rebellion, attacking the garrison of Derry. By the end of the ninth century the Dohertys were lords of the territory, according to the Annals of the Four Masters recorded in the Franciscan Abbey of Donegal town. The islet beyond

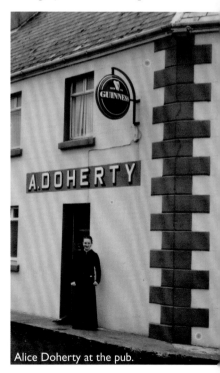

Alice Doherty at the pub.

29

Carrickbraghy is where the illegal potchin was brewed, and across the sea is the Mull of Kintyre and Scotland.

Further around the coast is Greencastle, another stronghold of the Doherty clan. We meet an American woman there and Jack tells her the history of this ruin on the banks of Lough Foyle. Like us, she prefers the castle ruins to the ones renovated for tourists, and is glad to have met someone who knows their history. We eat fish and chips at Greencastle. The crows are more polite than New Zealand seagulls and wait until we have finished our meal and are back in the car before they descend on the outdoor table for our crumbs. It is a beautiful drive home towards Derry along the shores of the Lough.

At last Ainslie, our much-awaited visitor from Featherston, is due at Belfast airport and we leave early in the morning to meet her. (Later in the day, the man who lives on our corner meets Jack and says, "Ooh, you were away early this morning and all". The neighbours don't miss a lot that goes on among these newcomers who open their windows, have bare feet and talk funny to the children who knock on the door for a chat.)

As we head through Derry over the Foyle River and on to Belfast, I know I have left the Republic because the green post offices are now painted red. The flags also indicate where I am. In Éire most of the flags tell me who the local Gaelic football club is, whereas in the north they fly either the green, orange and white Irish flag or the Union Jack, showing what community they belong to. I also notice an occasional blue and white Scottish flag.

Another clue to whether I am in the north or in the Republic is the names of the potatoes. On the day we arrived in Letterkenny I saw a roadside stall selling 'Fresh Queens'. We stopped to buy Golden Queen peaches. Instead we found Dublin Queen potatoes, known as Dublin Queens or just Queens.

In Northern Ireland I see potatoes for sale at the side of the road, but they are called British Queens. There are many subtle and not so subtle ways to supplement the information given by the map in the car.

We arrive at Belfast International Airport, where we see no sign of the army or police. This is a major change from my last visit. We eventually find Ainslie and decide to drive the long way home to Letterkenny around the glens of Antrim so we can see the north-east corner of Ireland.

'Carrickfergus' is the first song on the CD player as we head towards the town of the same name before driving through the nine glens, valleys with a village nestled in each, with stunning views at the tops of the hills from the road that winds around the coast. We stop for lunch on the brow of one hill that has a clear view all the way to Scotland, picnicking on our usual bread, cheese, crackers and clementines. Alice and I love the clementines, which we know as mandarins in New Zealand. We regularly include this new word in our conversations.

"Does anyone want a clementine?"

"Do we need to buy any clementines today?"

"These South African clementines are delicious."

We laugh when Jack asks if we have any "carolines" left.

Carrickbraghy Castle, County Donegal (also opposite).

Greencastle, County Donegal.

At the Giant's Causeway the rocks are five-sided and packed in tall vertical columns. The sea has eroded columns and left flat rocks to walk on. Their smooth, black, flat surfaces have ample space for your whole foot. The rocks fit together tightly, with no gaps in which to lose your footing. Directly across the sea is Scotland and Staffa Island, where the same rock formation is found. I stand in awe at creation. Together they provide a dramatic landscape for Ireland's famous stories about the giant Finn McCool and the Scottish giant Benandonner.

We climb the steep hill in hot sunshine listening to the thunder out at sea and by the time we arrive at the top, heavy raindrops are falling. On the way home we call at Dunluce Castle and drive past Bushmills, the world's oldest licensed distillery. Ainslie's stories of her time in Liverpool entertain us all the way home.

Ainslie is a nurse and dairy farmer in New Zealand, and she stayed next door to a farmer near Liverpool who milked 100 cows, all with computerised ear tags. The farmer had a printout available each day of how much milk the cows gave and how much grass and feed they were eating. If the readings were down he could investigate possible causes much sooner. His cowshed was called the parlour.

It was enlightening to tour Donegal with a dairy farmer in the car. Ainslie stopped to photograph an Irish farmer's 'crop' of ragwort to reassure her sons how clean their Featherston farm was in comparison. Ragwort is a noxious weed that farmers in both countries must control.

During Ainslie's visit we find we have to renew the rental car in Dublin; not possible by phone or email. This is an opportunity to show Ainslie more of the countryside that becomes a more extensive tour when we lose our way on the road to Dublin, and again on the return trip. Jack is turning more Irish by the minute, explaining, "It's not as if we are on the wrong road. I just don't think we are on the right one just now."

We are the only car on the road as we circle the roundabout before Strabane at 6.30 a.m. This used to be an ominous border point, but the buildings have been demolished and a grassed area created where several lamppost-tall sculptures stand made of steel strips moulded into figures playing music, including a fiddler, a flute player, a drummer and a singer. Through the thick fog, the bright early morning rays of sun dance on the musicians as we walk among them.

Newgrange is a compulsory visit for all our visitors to Ireland. Newgrange is 1000 years older than Stonehenge and 500 years older than the Egyptian pyramids. Standing in the chamber of this ancient place, where light enters on the day of the winter solstice, is always a humbling experience, combining an awareness of the power of science and creative artistry. How can I be standing inside this megalithic tomb, built in 3200 BC, where not a drop of water has penetrated since?

Music makers near Strabane.

In the carpark, a man with a cellphone appears beside our picnic. Someone has phoned asking for his help, and he is replying, "Well y'know, I moight be able to help you — but then again, I moight not, so ring me back if you get stuck!" I eavesdrop on both adults and children and their accent and turn of phrase captivate me.

We find our way to a carpark in central Dublin and climb on a Dublin city tour bus. This is a quick way to see Dublin and get your bearings, as you can hop on or off at the various stops and listen to the informative commentary by the driver, laced with wit and a few Irish songs. Today he includes 'Raindrops Keep Falling on My Head' just as the rain begins to fall on those of us sitting upstairs for better views.

In O'Connell Street, James Larkin, the founder of the Irish Trade Union movement, has his arms thrust out exhorting justice for

Newgrange entrance, County Meath.

workers. From the ground his statue is tall but from the top of the bus I am able to give him a nod of recognition for his indirect influence on the development of union health services in New Zealand for workers and families on low incomes, the field I had worked in before coming to Ireland. He nods back, to be sure.

The large maternity hospital in Dublin is called the Rotunda. A woman from Wexford has given birth to quins. Her parish has been praying for her and the babies every day for months. The headlines a couple of days later read: "Wexford Mother of Quins Adamant No Fertility Treatment Used." Months later, the Wexford quins will appear on *The Late, Late Show* on Friday night.

We are photographed with Molly Malone, the tart with the cart or the trollop with the scallops as the Dubliners call her, and wander up Grafton Street and into Temple Bar. There are plenty of trinkets on sale for St Patrick's Day, including green glittery headbands and long green, white and orange lolly sticks. We want to buy our friend Marie one of everything, knowing the fun she'll have on 17 March in New Zealand. We settle for a green bridal garter that plays the tune of 'When Irish Eyes are Smiling'.

It rains heavily so we eat early in an Italian restaurant. *Run By Real Italians* reads the sign in the window. Our umbrellas have been left in the car by mistake, so we shelter here and eventually manage to leave Dublin city as smoothly as we arrived.

On our way home to Letterkenny we stop to fill up with petrol, but the car won't start again. Nothing works. I find the manual, and the first troubleshooting step reads "Check you have the correct key." Jack discovers he has another key in his pocket which he has collected at the rental car office by mistake. Irish traffic signs take a more positive approach in modifying driver behaviour. Give Way becomes Yield and the road humps are called speed cushions.

At an army roadblock in Omagh we are asked stop and turn off our headlights. Six men, with two or three others behind them carrying rifles, are stopping and looking in cars. They wave us on. It is the anniversary of the 1998 Omagh bombing that killed twenty-nine, and an announcement has been made that there will be an inquiry into why the police never responded to the warning about the bomb.

We finally arrive home about 11.30. Our long day has included the stillness of ancient Newgrange and the bustle of Dublin. Ireland embraces both of these — and everything in between. This is what I love about this land.

Kiwi update, July

Over breakfast we toast with our cups of tea the Wellington book launch of Robert and Joanna Consedine's book about the Treaty of Waitangi, *Healing Our History.* My sister Claire will send us a newspaper report about the book launch, but I have yet to find the book itself in the Donegal bookshops. We would love to have been there; we have become so aware of correlations with Ireland's history, particularly after visiting Belfast to farewell Ainslie.

The postman delivers a letter from my friend Patsy. She has been writing to me for over forty years and this one is vintage material that brings me completely up-to-date with the social scene in Wellington, all that I am missing, and the goings-on in her household — in particular her granddaughter Moana's latest musings. The Irish postman has even figured out the meaning of 'Doherty whanau' as well.

Our mail has always presented challenges to the New Zealand postal service, as we often have visitors staying. When Jack had cancer, an old friend sent a get-well gift. The brown paper parcel arrived in our letterbox simply addressed to: "Jack Doherty, you know, that old bastard, somewhere in Featherston." Being Featherston, the package made it to the right person without any trouble and inside the parcel was a piece of 150 x 50mm timber with the get-well message scrawled on it. The Irish would easily understand our sense of extended family, if not the word 'whanau' itself.

Three
Hail Marys
for 'ewe'.

5

GARTAN AND GLENCOLUMBCILLE

Letterkenny is quiet on a Saturday morning at 11.30. The live music advertised in Market Square is a solitary man busking on an accordion. We amble up and down both sides of the street while Jack researches the 'traditional music' venues for the evening. Saturday night seems more a young person's band night, and one publican says to him, "Sure now, there'll be traditional music tonight, if yourself comes in and starts playing it!" Life here is never dull, and still holds daily surprises.

My friend Kath's dad is a Eugene Conaghan. I send her a newspaper cutting from the Donegal paper about a young Eugene Conaghan who is in court this week in Donegal. His lawyer, a Mr Doherty, explained Eugene's misdemeanours as "riotous behaviour caused by peer pressure". Kath and I have raised eleven children between us and this sounds like a realistic explanation for some of the Conaghan and Doherty clan behaviour in New Zealand!

The Heritage Centre on the shores of Lough Gartan has a display about St Colmcille, who was born near the lough and later founded the abbey in Iona, Scotland, in the sixth century. While in exile from Ireland he wrote:

I remember the sound of the wind
I remember the cuckoo calling
I remember the great stags leaping
I remember the blackbird crying

36

Glen Veagh eviction tapestries, Gartan.

Alice has gone for a run around the rhododendron-fringed lake edge, so I call her in to see the display of artwork. It includes a tapestry made by the women of Letterkenny, telling the story of the Glen Veagh evictions in 1861. The landlord, John Adair, and closed the school with 30 children on the roll, and ordered the soldiers to destroy the houses. Many of the families fled to Perth, Western Australia, and their names embroidered on the last tapestry are all familiar: Rodden (my great-grandfather's name), Doherty, Curran, Conaghan and Friel.

The exhibition also includes an intricate lace tapestry of the Gartan parish, with wildflowers embroidered for the families of the parish that are named. The lace, the background material and the embroidery are all in white. There are also six panels of the 'Our Father' cross-stitched in the six Celtic languages.

During Ainslie's visit, we drive across to see Jack's cousin Eileen and her husband Frank in Irvinestown, Fermanagh. Their son Brian, who has been living in New Zealand, is over from Scotland, and our niece Liz Doherty has arrived from Dublin. It is quite a reunion. Irvinestown is the village where Jack's granddad first worked after leaving school. We see the shop again, now named Maguires, and enjoy Frank's photos of their New Zealand trip and the Doherty family reunion Jack organised at Days Bay three years earlier. Eileen and Frank's hospitality has been shared many times over with New Zealand Dohertys and their children, and they are always warm and welcoming.

On our way home from Irvinestown we hear on the car radio of a reported theft in Dublin. Over 200 blocks have been removed from the Liffey River wall. These valuable Wicklow stones, worth about £750,000, have disappeared in the middle of the night and no one can solve the mystery, though huge earth-moving

Caldragh Cemetery, Boa Island, County Fermanagh.

machinery would have been necessary to uplift them. Even the radio announcer is obviously stunned.

Also on the way home we visit Boa Island to see the Janus Stone and the other ancient stones that stand, still and mysterious, in the long summer grass and among the wildflowers of the Caldragh cemetery.

A visit to Glencolumbcille in west Donegal takes you through the town of Ardara. Three tractors with silage trailers are stuck in the hilly main street, providing another photo opportunity for Ainslie the dairy farmer.

In the bogs on top of the Donegal plains peat is packed tightly in long lines of plastic bags, waiting to dry. This is not as attractive as the triangular piles of turf you see in some places, but it is more efficient for drying. The sweet, distinctive scent fills the car when you drive past a house where a peat fire burns.

The Janus Stone, Boa Island.

Hay is rolled in black polythene bales similar to those in New Zealand, but I also notice triangular or round haystacks made with a pitchfork. By the gap in a hedge an old man stands in a suit jacket and black cap holding a bulky bundle of freshly cut hay under each arm. A delightful-looking Irish combine-harvester, he is waiting to cross the lane.

The sheep in Donegal have graceful black faces and long curly horns — and often have red or blue chalk marks on their backs. When I approach they don't scatter and run straight into a fence like New Zealand sheep, but look up as if to say "Here's another tourist tracing their Irish ancestors." Grazing in the middle of a country road beside a statue of Mary and Bernadette, they sit completely still, posing nonchalantly for my photo.

At Glencolumbcille a long, steep walk leads to the white sandy beach of Tramore Strand. We are planning a picnic lunch on the seat halfway down the track, until Jack discovers he has left the lunch on the table at home. Ainslie looks in disbelief at the flimsy, torn, foot-and-mouth protection mat on the track. How could a scrap of sodden carpet defend Ireland's farming industry?

In the absence of lunch, we find a tearoom in a village of thatched cottages that includes a school museum and discover that in 1878 Hannah Doherty, along with several other Dohertys, was on the school roll.

Back around the coast we stop in the fishing village of Killybegs, where dozens of gaily painted fishing boats are anchored. The boys from Killybegs, as the song says, have obviously come rolling home.

Donegal town is busy with summer tourists shopping and we enjoy the craic — Irish for fun or light-hearted mischief — with George who owns a gift shop.

Tramore Strand, and below, Glencolumbcille.

I find a hat I like and declare it can be an early birthday present but George is worried about the time lag. "Ooh, I don't know Jack. Now September is an awfully long way off, y'know — a long time for herself to wait for a hat!"

George's mother was a Doherty so he deducts 99p off the hat and wonders if we know his friend working in plastics in Auckland. He gives out about the Germans living in Donegal accessing the rent subsidies and poaching salmon, and not working seven days a week like himself. George ends our riotous visit by exclaiming, "You know Jack, being a Doherty, you should've told me when you first came in and I would've known I was dealing with aristocracy right from the start." Then nodding at me, he adds, "Does herself there know that in Ireland if you're spinning a yarn with a lot of bullshit in it, they say, 'Ooh, your granny was a Doherty and your aunty a Maguire'!" When I think of the number of Dohertys and Maguires in my life back in New Zealand, this is a gem to remember. We promise George we will bring our Kiwi visitors back to see him.

One gift shop sells navy-blue pottery mugs and plates with koru-like swirls, and we find Alice a striking celtic design silver bracelet. She has been patient as we meander and stop and look at everything and everyone, including Donegal Castle and the nearby river mouth.

On Ainslie's last evening we visit Gallagher's Hotel in Letterkenny for dinner and an evening of traditional music. The music begins with a couple of men on the guitar and violin but they are soon joined by another on the banjo, a girl playing the tin whistle and the violin and her sister on the accordion. After dinner when we are in the bar listening to the music and enjoying the four old coves sitting over their pints, the waitresses come in with bowls of steaming Irish stew to feed all the patrons.

On the windowsill in the kitchen I have a glass of flowers: two types of heather, one pale pink and one purple, some green ferns and a bunch of purple thistles. Not many of the locals have gardens as we know them in New Zealand, but the spring bulbs are for sale in the shops so if we manage to find work and stay, I will plant some just to keep me grounded. I remember planting bulbs down the driveway of the farm just before we left Te Wakaiti, and again on the deck at Sunshine Bay the autumn my Uncle Jack got sick. They keep my spirits alive and in spring bright

People of the land

for Jack

The thought
Of our ancestors
Lying together

In the earth
Of Donegal

Feels as right
As knowing
How it will be
Lying together
With you

In the earth
Of Aotearoa

The land always remains

yellow daffodils appearing early is one of the things I look forward to most and always celebrate.

A windy storm today has left branches on the road. It was the talk of Clachan Mor, our street, with cousin Irene exclaiming "Ooh, Mother of God Almighty, it was enough to put hairs on an elephant!" The time is passing and every day we check to see if the All Blacks test tickets are on sale for the November game in Dublin. We are trying to buy nine tickets for Kiwis over here, and must supply a New Zealand passport number for each ticket.

Finally I receive an email from a recruitment agency in Dublin asking if my job application is still valid as they are short-listing this week for interviews. "Definitely yes," I reply. I hope to hear this week about the next stage. For some reason I think it sounds hopeful.

There will be implications if we are to be Dublin-based. Although having no work has meant we can explore all of Donegal and the Inishowen Peninsula and learn the Doherty clan history, our money is rapidly running out.

Kiwi update, August

When Thomas David McPadden, my new nephew, is born in New Zealand we receive the news as we are leaving to go to Eileen and Frank's house in Fermanagh for dinner. When we return home later in the evening, my sister Gid has sent his photo around the world, and he is online in Donegal at twelve hours old. When I speak to my brother Paul, baby Tom is due to go home to big sister Millie, who is apparently non-committal apart from saying, "Tom's out now," whenever the new baby is mentioned.

Claire, my sister, emails me to say she had a visit from a tui which had flown in her garden the morning he was born, and she called out, "Yes, I know you have a new little grandson!" My mother's name was Tui, and we are very aware of the tui that appear at significant times in our family. Among these times was the day we moved house to Sunshine Bay; whenever I am with my mother's favourite niece, Janice; during Hannah's wedding when Uncle Ross blessed the rings with an olive branch from the tree that my mother had planted at Te Wakaiti, our community farm; and now on this morning of Thomas's birth.

I look outside and Donegal feels unfamiliar, the Irish crows no substitute for the tui of Aotearoa.

6

Poster of the hunger strikers.

BELFAST AND KILMACRENNAN

After farewelling Ainslie at Belfast airport, Jack takes us for "just a quick look" around Belfast and we manage to get lost driving through the Catholic and Protestant areas of this complex city. It is the twentieth anniversary of the 1981 hunger strikes. Posters and murals commemorate the men who died. The posters are mounted on a large black capital letter H for the H Block (Maze) prison where they died, demanding the status of political prisoners from Margaret Thatcher. Women are often the invisible victims in war and I thought of the mammys, wives, girlfriends, sisters and daughters of these men and their suffering at the time and over the two decades since. Some of the women were imprisoned as well.

A report has just been released on restructuring the Northern Ireland police force to ensure it is more impartial. The Catholic bishops are supporting it. Sinn Féin says it doesn't go far enough. The GAA (Gaelic Athletic Association) has been urged to repeal clause 21 that states any member of the GAA is banned from joining the RUC (Royal Ulster Constabulary), and so it goes on. As we enter Belfast past Templepatrick I notice the Union Jack flying on the fence in front of the police station. Impartiality may take time, I think.

The murals of Belfast are graphic and poignant. The exposed end wall of a row of houses is often painted with a mural and accompanying words that tell the history or the future for the community that lives there. For example:

Our revenge will be the laughter of our children.
Everyone, Republican or otherwise, has his or her own particular role to play, no matter how big or small.
They may kill the revolutionary, but never the revolution.
Language rights are human rights.
Remember the martyrs who died in H Block on Hunger Strike.

I will plan a slower and more relaxed visit to Belfast, as today I am tense and unsure of my ground and unable to pop in and out of the car with my camera, like a Japanese tourist might in Queenstown, New Zealand. It must be emotional for the artists and for those whose homes the murals are painted on. But it is also emotional for me, a Kiwi with Irish ancestors who were forced to leave their homeland because of hunger and colonisation.

Earlier in the week we saw a remarkable TV documentary about Belfast and the Troubles. On the night we return from Belfast the next programme in the series screens and is about the political mural art of Belfast, showing the murals of both sides and co-operative murals from today's young people. While there are signs of momentous change for the people of Northern Ireland, the injustices of the past are not forgotten, so it is hard to imagine immediate peace. We don't see any army or police presence in Belfast though — in itself a major change.

I enjoyed Belfast. It is spacious and open without the crowds and traffic of Dublin or Derry. We drive around the dockyards where the *Titanic* was built, looking for the pub called the Rotterdam which still has the handcuffs where the convicts were held while waiting to board the ship to Australia. Convicts like Michael in the song 'The Fields of Athenry', who gets shipped to Botany Bay for stealing Trevelyn's corn "so the young might see the morn".

This is Alice's favourite Irish song. We play it every day as we travel, as well as Jack's song about Derry, 'The Town I Loved So Well'. Both songs tell the history of Ireland forcefully, one is from my great-grandparents' time, when they left Ireland, and the other is about Derry's more recent history. Both songs make me weep whenever I hear them.

H Block Remembrance, Belfast.

The State Opera House in Belfast is grand, and Jack shows us the Europa Hotel where he stayed eight years earlier, when it had the dubious reputation of being Europe's most bombed hotel. The day after he left it was bombed again, so he returned to take a photo showing the windows missing from the five lower floors. Belfast today is much more peaceful.

When you drive to Belfast from Derry you cross the Foyle Bridge that spans Lough Foyle. It is broad and long and I was thinking quietly what a strategic position the bridge has in the North. On our return from Belfast airport four hours later, the same Foyle Bridge is closed. It takes over an hour to manoeuvre our way through the traffic jam in Derry. Once home, we hear a news report that police found a bomb on the Foyle Bridge that afternoon, and have closed the bridge for two days. I am more relaxed living over the border in Southern Ireland.

The news also carries a report that the GAA football and hurling grounds in the North are being planted with bombs. The niggling is constant and seems to be on the increase. Some of the priests have come out angrily slamming the Catholic bishops' premature approval of the police restructuring report, saying "We have no Helda Camaras or Oscar Romeros among our bishops!" Helda Camara and Oscar Romero were South American bishops who heroically supported the liberation of their people, becoming martyrs for the cause.

We spend the next morning working on further job applications and housework before driving to Fanad Head, the topmost western point of the Lough Swilly peninsula that looks across to Inishowen. The views are spectacular and the day is warm and sunny. The beach at Portsalon rivals the golden sand of Totaranui in the Abel Tasman National Park in New Zealand, where we have enjoyed several family holidays. While Jack visits the heritage centre in Rathmullen to read the history at the 'Flight of the Earls' exhibition, Alice and I decide to explore Rathmullen, and find enchanting old postcards of Donegal in a secondhand shop.

On our way home we visit the Kilmacrennan cemetery where the Roddens are buried. They are my great-grandmother's family and lie beside many Dohertys. The cemetery is also the site of the abbey, built by the Friel family. It is where the religious ceremony to anoint the O'Donnell chiefs was held; the civil ceremony took place at the holy well at Doon Rock. It is moving to think of our ancestors living so close together and lying together in this burial ground, and to think that so many miles and years away in New Zealand, Jack and I met and are spending our lives together.

Our car radio reports a huge traffic jam in Dublin; a combine harvester has broken down and is blocking an entire main street. The week has also seen over 2000 jobs lost in the IT market, including 100 in Gweedore, Donegal. Locals comment that Donegal and Inishowen missed out on many of the benefits during the economic boom and they are worried about the impact of such a dramatic downturn. "It's like watching a set of dominoes falling," they say. Just as in Donegal, the residents of Dublin north of the Liffey feel limited benefits. The Dublin northsiders refer to the Celtic Tiger as the 'Mangy Cat'.

Our niece Liz is here again from Dublin, her bus finally arriving after long delays caused by traffic jams near Slane Castle where U2 are performing. Liz is relieved to see the improved demeanour of her aunty, uncle and cousin. She is saying her goodbyes to Ireland before returning to New Zealand. We visit Ballybofey for a night in the Claddagh Bar, where traditional music is advertised from 10 p.m. It's all quiet when we arrive at 10.30 and the barman comes over at 11.15, saying, "You moight tink dat de band is just late, but oi don't tink it's coming at all."

Early next morning we drive Liz to Buncrana to see the Doherty Keep and climb the steep hill through the Gap of Mamore and to Malin Head to see the rest of the Inishowen Peninsula. The peninsula was Doherty clan land before Queen

Liz and Jack, Buncrana.

Elizabeth I gave it to Sir Arthur Chichester — a gesture unappreciated by every Doherty at the time and ever since. The weather is perfect and the views over the land and coast of Donegal are majestic.

A few men sit alongside us at the bar of the Arch Inn as we watch the All Blacks beat South Africa. They are impressed with the weather on the screen! Towards half-time the barman asks if the channel can be changed for a live horse race. One of the patrons has a thousand pounds on a horse. A man named McLoughlin tells Jack that all Dohertys are horse 'teeves', and Jack defends his clan, saying they're better than the McLouglins who take the lot — horses, land, everything. At least the Dohertys are only interested in the horses. It's great craic for the afternoon and the rugby game quickly becomes secondary.

We buy a lottery ticket at Paul Doherty's newsagent in Carndonagh and arrange to watch the replay of the All Blacks test at the Arch Inn. About six shops are named Doherty in this village.

The *Between the Jigs and Reels* concert in the new theatre in Letterkenny is an evening of Donegal music, song, poetry and drama. The accordion player Mairtin O'Connor is fantastic as are two fine fiddlers and an engaging percussionist who reminds Alice and me of our friend Peter, who lives across the harbour from us in

Wellington. The songs are mainly in Gaelic. The poetry is about Donegal and Colmcille, and the drama an excerpt from one of Brian Friel's plays, *Translations*. The theatre is large and modern and a valuable asset to Letterkenny and County Donegal with a programme of drama, music and opera for the months ahead.

Carndonagh newsagent.

46

We have been hearing reports today that the Catholic Church is concerned about the introduction of the euro in case Catholics continue to put a single coin in the collection plate. In real terms this will mean a dramatic drop in takings. However, Father O'Sullivan from Kerry is quoted as saying his brilliant solution to this potential disaster is for all Catholics to put two of the new euro coins in the plate!

Alice lobbies hard to get us to tune into the FM station on the car radio, as Jack and I relish every talkback call and news item like this one. We take turns and play our favourite CDs for variety, but the entertainment and craic of the radio callers is funny with clever hosts facilitating the exquisite communication process.

Kiwi update, August

An email has arrived from Jack's cousin Pip telling us we will be missing their "farewell to the old carpet party and Pip and Pat's 93rd birthday". The party is to precede the arrival of the new carpet. I have suggested they send a relic of the old carpet to the homeland. Next week our friend Mike Fitzsimons is launching *With a Passion*, the book about passionate New Zealanders that he and colleague Nigel Beckford have written. Surprisingly, it omits Jack Doherty's passion about the Doherty clan history of Inishowen, Donegal.

This morning the postman delivers a wonderful letter from our friend Lynette telling us of Luke and Nuala's radio programme. Our daughter Hannah sends a tui card with daphne flowers in plastic wrap. The envelope holds the beautiful daphne scent of early spring in New Zealand.

I often chat with my sisters online and this morning Claire, Gid, Ma and I have a long conversation, with several threads happening together. I find it a useful remedy for homesickness and a lot of fun, especially towards the end when we are all saying goodbye and trying to have the last word.

Tory Island, County Donegal.

7

TORY ISLAND

After a day trip to Tory Island, seven miles west of the Donegal coastline, we are all sunburned. The weather forecasters here often predict "cloudy with patches of sunshine", which differs from the frequent New Zealand forecast for "patches of rain". Today patches of sunshine were everywhere as we caught the small ferry, overflowing with people of all ages chatting in Gaelic.

Tory Island is unique. More than two decades ago the Irish government tried to move the Islanders to the mainland but they resisted. Today Tory has a population of 150, electricity, a new school block, a new pier, and a flourishing tourist industry with £4 million spent recently on the hotel.

Two main groups of houses are scattered along the island, with a lighthouse at one end and a white cottage at the other. Jack spends half an hour at the cottage with the two old men who live there. In their lounge filled with pipe smoke so thick they can hardly be seen, they tell him that the best thing about Tory Island, and the reason people come from all over is "to get the lovely fresh air". One of them says incredulously, over and over, "Noo Zealand t, t, t, Noo Zealand t,t,t,t!" The other old man asks about the weather and the fishing.

Alice, Liz and Jack bike across the pink heather and soft bogs of the island where the road runs out. I sit on a rock in the sun and finish my novel.

Tory Island was the fort of Balor, the one-eyed demi-god and chief of one of the ancient warrior groups known as the Formonians. His fort, Dun Bahalor, is the rock formation at the eastern end of the island.

Jack's cousins Margaret and Tommy, both over 80, travel to Tory with us and members of the Letterkenny historical society. It's Margaret's first trip to the island. On the way back to the mainland we are surprised when lifejackets are handed out to everyone. Alice thinks she's on the *Titanic*. We try to appear calm but we are curious. Though the boat is packed with babies and old people, everyone else seems jovial and relaxed. It turns out that when the tide is low the boat can't berth at the pier on the mainland, so we have to put on our lifejackets, climb down a rope ladder into a small boat and be transported to shore. It's quite an adventure for Margaret, who announces she won't be going back to Tory Island.

Unlike the blue Pacific, the Atlantic is mottled with shades of black and grey and looks like diluted ink. If grief had a colour perhaps this would be it.

Returning from Tory Island, we stop for chips down by the river in Bunbeg before calling in at the Doon Rock and the well. Kitty, a girl with tight ringlet curls and a long pink dress, dances around the well like a fairy. Her grandparents and two great-aunties walk around the well in their bare white feet saying their prayers. Kitty starts to play with the mementos hanging in the trees. She touches the rosary beads, toys, money, photos, letters and ribbons and calls excitedly in her Irish voice: "Ooh look, Granny! Here is baby Matthew's dummy."

Balor's minders

As Atlantic swells subdue
Seabirds fill the aura
Of this ancient island
Nest of myth and legend

Eastwards lies your Dun
Prominent, separate, unreachable
The dark home of cormorants
I stand in awe

Sleeping upturned currachs
Mark your neighbour's boundary
I ask them of your whereabouts
They hide the secrets of antiquity

Their silence thrills this visitor
Music of Tory, play on

Jack Doherty

Tory Island shrine to Mary.

Granny calls Kitty over to the well and rubs the holy water on her hands, telling the girl to pray, "Now please God take away my warts." Kitty entertains us, her grandparents smiling and enjoying her free spirit while they continue their barefoot prayers.

Yesterday was a day for Irish cousins to visit us. Eileen from Irvinestown came with her sister Teresa and Teresa's son, Garvan. Teresa wore her New Zealand T-shirt especially for us. Later that same evening, Margaret and Tommy came to watch the Rose of Tralee competition finals on TV. They were surprised we knew of the competition and that New Zealand was always represented.

Jack, Margaret, Eileen and Teresa's grandparents are all siblings, and Margaret and Tommy have lived in Letterkenny for sixty years. I think we are a new project for them and when Margaret invites us for Sunday dinner she adds, "Come about 1.15. I can't for the love of God work out why it hasn't happened sooner!"

Tommy and Margaret Kelly.

One evening, the Clachan Mor Residents Association gather for the tidying up of the estate. Our cul-de-sac of twenty-two houses is quiet, and the road and grounds around the houses are in mint condition. We have been asked to arrive at 6.30 with a brush and a black bag. Initially only the men are there, with about twenty children on their bikes. The oldest, and the leader of the street, is thirteen-year-old Amanda, who knows everything and everyone. She sells us a raffle ticket for a car, telling us the proceeds will help fund a counsellor for those with breast cancer. Amanda asks if we are from Australia, why we are here and how long we will be living in the street.

When the women appear I go out and met her parents, who live on the corner, and the family who run the B&B at the entrance to our street. The three-year-old twins from across the road are there, and Mrs Doherty from next door and her daughter Marie. It is a great community scene, with some arriving just as we finish. There is little to do and apparently it is the first event the street has held. Maybe it's to meet the new ones with the funny accents in number fourteen as we are busily interviewed all evening and made welcome.

Mt Errigal in Donegal is similar in shape and winter colour to Mt Taranaki in New Zealand. Today is the first time we've seen it so clear and free of cloud or mist.

We decide to climb the 751-metre peak, and will no doubt debate forever whose effort is the best. Jack climbs all of it, and Alice at least two-thirds. I am going quite steadily until I hit the crumbly rock. I was much happier in the soft bog that was bouncy like a trampoline, especially the parts when I sank right down. It is less gruelling than the peak Jack and my sister Claire climbed at Lake Rotoiti in the South Island at Easter, and Jack comments several times, "Claire would love this one!"

The talkback topics today are the shortage of student accommodation and tips from listeners about how to meet "looovly young women". It is entertainment plus, especially the Galway woman giving out about the student boarder who ate her out of house and home. He wanted more than four fish fingers every Friday night along with his potatoes and beans, and was often at home instead of out at university.

When the student asked her how much the lettuce cost in his salad sandwiches, herself had replied, "I wouldn't be wasting my feckin' money buying tomatoes and ham and cheese to put in with your lettuce." He only lasted five weeks, the last straw being when the student's dad phoned to ask if his son was studying and herself replied: "As if I care a feck whether he's studying or not. He's eating me out of house and home — that's what he's doing!" She ended her call to the radio with, "Jesus Mary and Blessed St Joseph, this all happened on a Friday and I said to your man, you'll be gone by Monday! Never again would I have a student boarder, never ever again, God Almighty, NO!"

Our frequent outings in the car give us plenty of opportunity to listen to talkback. Siobhan Devlin has arrived from Dublin to spend the last days of her three-month school holidays, and we are driving with her in the pouring rain to Dungloe, the home town of singer Daniel O'Donnell, where the annual 'Mary of Dungloe' competition is held. I prefer a stauncher approach to Irish music myself, like that of the Pogues, but Daniel O'Donnell has a strong following both in Ireland and internationally.

Dungloe is wet and cold. We will return on a finer day, as the harbour and coastal route look attractive through the mist. No doubt we will be entertained once again as we drive by the outrageous claims and the unconscious humour of talkback callers.

Another day we watch the All Blacks play Australia in the second Bledisloe Cup game in Gallagher's pub in Letterkenny. We order a full Irish breakfast, the classic Ulster fry-up, and wait for kick-off. When the pub opens at 10 there are about nine men at the bar waiting for their first morning pint, all with their backs to the TV. Alice, Jack and I are the only ones watching the rugby; the men only look up from their pints for the haka or when Jonah Lomu appears. The game is frustrating

Toilet sign, Tory Island.

Mt Errigal, County Donegal.

and disappointing to watch, but Alice remarks how good it is to see faces in the crowd that are familiar.

Later we receive in-depth match reports from our friend Martin Maguire, suggesting he and Jack get their jerseys out again. There's also one from my sister Claire, suggesting Anton Oliver (the New Zealand hooker) was throwing the lineout ball directly to John Eales the Australian captain, because he felt sorry for him playing his last game for Australia.

But what does stir the locals is the World Cup soccer match in which Ireland defeats Holland. This is a fantastic win for the underdogs and the crowd goes crazy singing 'The Fields of Athenry'. Goal scorer Jason McInteer is the hero, and the coach Mick McCarthy interviewed straight after the game, threatens to show his bum in Byrne's shop window if Jason McInteer doesn't get a football club contract out of this.

After eight weeks of living in Donegal, one of our sturdiest tent pegs is removed. Alice is returning to New Zealand. It has been a huge decision for all three of us. Going to school in Letterkenny is not going to work for Alice, so she is returning to spend six months with her older sister Hannah, and Michael, and six months with big brother Josh, and Roze. She will enjoy Year 13 back at home with all her friends.

Margaret and Tommy have told us about the Bridge of Tears in Donegal, Droichead na nDeor, where families would travel with their children who were emigrating to America, Britain, Australia and New Zealand. From this bridge near Muckish Mountain, the Donegal emigrants would travel alone to Derry to board their ship. I tell Alice we will go there in September when she returns to New Zealand.

In the meantime, I am distracted by news that Australia is ignoring refugees in boats off their coast, but New Zealand and Nauru, that other speck in the Pacific, are responding. And Donald Woods, the white South African journalist who in exile wrote *Biko: Cry Freedom*, has died in England. Steve Biko's son has travelled from South Africa with his mother and sisters to speak at the funeral. Woods' book was one of my early consciousness-raisers about apartheid and made me aware of New Zealand's responsibility in regard to rugby tours and the need for us to exert direct pressure on the South African government to review their racist policies.

Just as I am wondering if the Irish post is nothing but a black hole, I receive notification of a job interview in Dublin. We have by now exhausted local possibilities and applied for a couple of jobs in Dublin. But we have also booked our flights to return home with Alice, and will only stay here if we do secure employment. This would mean a two-month holiday in Donegal instead of the one or two-year visit we've planned, but our money has almost gone and our options feel limited.

Travelling people

for Jack

Your parents travelled like gypsies
Boarding a ferry to live on an island
Swapping the *Taranaki Daily Mail*
For swimming, fishing and walking

We came to see them,
Young again and happy
A short but treasured time
Before permanent farewells took place
For everyone

Your grandparents travelled too
From fear and poverty
And hunger
To Aotearoa
A future of children and grandchildren

Permanent farewells don't skip generations
Ask the mammys in Ireland
They danced on the crossroads
And sang their laments
Premature and forever

We hear their cries in Ireland
Homeland
Even today

Kiwi update, September

Jude, our son, is an avid snowboarder, and sends two text messages from Mt Ruapehu. The first one reads: "My last weekend up the mountain — I have met air and it likes me!" followed by another later in the day, "Walking down Ruapehu, brilliant day snowboarding, off to spa." Josh reassures me the snow is too soft and plentiful for major fractures.

Jessica, our daughter, is flatting 500 metres from Bondi Beach in Sydney and has work on a project changing the street numbers of all the residential addresses in Sydney. Her five Irish and English flatmates tease her about her Kiwi accent. When the plumbing needs fixing, the tradesman who arrives on the doorstep is an Irishman called Doherty, originally from Letterkenny!

Spring has arrived in New Zealand, and people are writing to us about freesias and daffodils.

The sweet peas here in Donegal are vivid in colour and scent, and dark pink hydrangeas, gladioli and outdoor begonias are everywhere. It is also peat harvesting time, and a worried Emmett in Dublin is trying to ripen his tomatoes in the waning sun. I reluctantly begin to acknowledge the early signs of autumn.

8

ARDOYNE AND BLOODY SUNDAY

I cry today, watching the footage on TV about school children in Ardoyne, Belfast. They are trying to walk to school and are being obstructed by violent abuse, protests and, yesterday, a bomb. Today the situation is improving, but the five- and six-year-olds are still walking past armoured cars, soldiers and Protestant men blowing whistles and sirens, many with their backs to the children. One explanation offered is that because the Protestants were banned by police from marching through the Catholic area in the July marching season, they are now not allowing the Holy Cross children access to the school up their road. An alternative entrance without police or army protection is being targeted as well. Parents and grandparents are escorting the children in an attempt to provide protection and security.

It is upsetting to see the ugly behaviour of the adults and to catch glimpses of the horror and terror on the faces of the children. Today there are reports of death threats against Catholic parents, and the situation is tense. It has the potential to either escalate into civil war again, or to bring people to their senses. Two days ago a Catholic woman was charged with deliberately killing a twelve-year-old boy, knocking him off his bicycle after rocks were thrown at her car.

A week later I read an interview with the principal of Holy Cross School in Ardoyne. The school is across the road from the local Protestant school, and the two schools have developed positive relationships over recent years, sharing classes and educational resources. During the protests Protestant parents have brought gifts and flowers to Holy Cross, offering their love and prayers and expressing shame at the "goings on of others" at the school gates. But this ray of hope gets no international media coverage.

My friend Patsy, an inspiring teacher at Holy Cross School in Wellington, tells me the children in her class have written to the children at Holy Cross in Ardoyne. One girl has written, "I hope you can learn to say, 'Please stop it — I don't like what you are doing'."

A general practitioner from Ardoyne has said that many of the children are now on tranquillisers and sleeping pills. I agree with Gerry Adams, leader of Sinn Féin, who says that even a silent protest targeting children is completely unacceptable.

Campbells gift shop in Ardara is owned by Hugh and his beautiful old mammy Philomena, who sell Irish crafts to the tourists. When Philomena appears with her long white hair and crinkly, smiling eyes, she is talking in Irish and dressed in an apron and oversized sneakers. When we see the newspaper photo of the children in Ardoyne trying to get to school she grips my arm tightly and says, "The troubles in the North will never go away."

Hugh can discuss rugby forever and knows more about New Zealand's latest selections than we do, entertaining us with the story of his winnings after betting £1000 on Australia in the recent rugby test against the All Blacks. As we leave the shop laden with jerseys and T-shirts, Hugh adds an Irish rugby jersey "for your man there" and a few spare T-shirts for any "babbies in the family". The best way to describe Hugh and Philomena's gift shop in Ardara is to say that "the craic was ninety" meaning much laughter and fun took place there.

Alice stays home to pack her bags the day that Jack, Margaret, their daughter Irene and I join the historical society tour of places in the life of Colmcille. We have already explored it all ourselves, but this time Margaret, who has a vast memory of Irish history, is able to fill in a few gaps along with the guest speakers at each site. As she says to Jack, "This place is heavin' with history."

We begin at the well of Ethne, a holy woman and a healer, who was Colmcille's mother. A prophecy from Ethne's well says that if you see two strange women there on three consecutive days, the world is going to end. I write to Phaidra Ethne back in New Zealand to tell her and her lovely grandmother, another Ethne, about the Irish Ethne and how special their name is.

The well is soon to undergo archaeological exploration — there is a circle of huge stones around the perimeter. Just before you reach the well, behind the churchyard, is a graveyard for souls in limbo. As children we were taught that limbo is the mysterious place you hang about in for eternity if you die before you are baptised. Until recently all stillborn or newborn babies who died in Ireland were buried in unconsecrated graves like this. It would be healing for the families if the church could now consecrate these separated burial grounds, given that limbo no longer officially exists.

The heritage tour seems to go on forever, through the narrow country lanes. Irene comments, "You're in Ireland now and the man who made time, made plenty of it." I will need to think carefully before passing on this gem to my friends Patsy, Marie and Kath, infamous for their Irish timekeeping.

Margaret's knee is troubling her so we wait as Jack and Irene climb the fences to cross the fields. Speaking of her daughter Irene, Margaret says, "Oh to be sure Jewarne, she's the best God ever put breath into." When the Angelus comes on the car radio at 6 p.m., Margaret stops mid-sentence, blesses herself and bows her head to pray the Angelus for a minute or two before resuming our conversation.

They announce on the radio the results of the Irish Strong Man competition for sheep throwing. It is unclear whether the sheep are dead or alive, but no doubt animal rights groups will respond before too long.

It is difficult to order lamb at restaurants here because of the shortage after the foot-and-mouth scare. I have seen a leg of lamb in the supermarket for the equivalent of $NZ80.

Jack is reading *Paddy Bogside*, the book about Derry written by Paddy Doherty. This particular Paddy Doherty was the man who welcomed "the boy home to Derry" when Jack visited with the Commonwealth group eight years earlier. Paddy had noticed there was a Doherty on the list and asked him to stand so he could especially welcome him home to Derry, the city of the Dohertys. This was a particularly emotional and defining moment for Jack, who has worked on Treaty of Waitangi issues for many years in New Zealand and knows the importance of knowing your turangawaewae (your place to stand).

When next we visit Derry, Jack spends a few hours with Paddy 'Bogside' Doherty, a colourful character, a born storyteller with a hopeful story to relate. He has been a leader and inspiration for the inner-city restoration project. Young unemployed Catholic and Protestants worked together to rebuild Derry after the destruction and bombing, and learned literacy and numeracy skills at the same time.

We walk the walls of the city looking at the housing areas with the Republican murals and flags on the Bogside, and the Loyalist murals and flags on the other side.

The Bloody Sunday Centre is flanked by two blue banners at the doors, one saying *Truth* and the other *Justice*. There is a slide show about that Sunday in January 1974 when the British army opened fire on a civil rights march, killing fourteen and injuring several others, all young men or fathers, one with eight children. The bloodstained Derry Civil Rights Association banner used to cover the bodies has never been washed and hangs on one wall of the centre. A photographic gallery and brief biographies of the victims tell of their families, their hobbies and careers.

The bloodstained Derry Civil Rights Association banner, from Bloody Sunday 1974.

Bloody Sunday posters.

Vivid posters tell the story of the search for truth and justice.

The road to truth, justice, reconciliation and healing is being travelled slowly since Tony Blair announced the new Saville inquiry in 1998. The earlier inquiry by Lord Widgery refused to acknowledge the 500 eyewitness accounts or any evidence that pointed to army culpability. "He found the innocent guilty and the guilty innocent" in the words of a Catholic bishop at the time. Although the coroner wrote that there was no doubt it was absolute murder, Lord Widgery described the actions of the army as "reckless shooting."

We cross the cobblestone courtyard from the Doherty tower to the handsome brick Guild Hall and spend two hours at the Bloody Sunday inquiry. Our bags are scanned by security and our camera removed, and we sit upstairs overlooking the court area, as you can in the New Zealand Parliament. One stained-glass window in the hall has Australia at the top of the frame and New Zealand and Newfoundland in the bottom corners.

Two women give evidence and recall that Sunday nearly thirty years ago. One, Margaret, is now sixty-five and her husband was a marshal on the march. When the shooting started she opened her front door to offer shelter. They were crammed in everywhere.

The court scene, with its PowerPoint presentations and statements on screens, must be intimidating for these women. The lawyers representing the soldiers cross-examine Margaret, who is resolute about what she saw on the "worst day of her life". At one stage, staring at the soldiers' lawyer, she said, "It doesn't matter how you might want me to describe it — whether they were on the edge of the footpath or the edge of the road or whether the coat was pale fawn or not. The men weren't moving because they were dead. They had been shot and that's what I heard and saw. That's what I remember."

The other woman had a four-week-old baby at the time, and was visiting her parents. When the shooting started they all hit the floor, and she remembered her new baby in her pram. She crawled down the hallway to get her.

Towards the end of her evidence, the lawyer representing the soldiers asks if she knew a Red Mickey Doherty very well.

"No," she replies, adding that the only Doherty she knew well was Patrick Doherty, one of the men killed on Bloody Sunday.

"But you have heard of, or know a little of Red Mickey Doherty?" he continues.

"Yes, I have seen him round," she says.

"When would that be?"

"Ooh, I couldn't tell ye, could be a while ago now."

"A decade or two ago? " he asks.

"Oh no, about a month ago I saw him in the city centre," she replies.

"Where is he now?" the lawyer persists.

She says, "You know, there are many Red Mickey Dohertys around Derry and I need to know we are talking about the same Red Mickey Doherty because we might be talking about different ones, you know. The one I am talking about, Red Mickey Doherty, is in my age group, maybe a little older than myself."

"No further questions," says the lawyer. He sits down, resigned. I'm not sure if his Red Mickey Doherty is the same as hers, but local knowledge seems to be an advantage.

It is moving being at the Bloody Sunday inquiry, and I try to imagine our own mothers might have coped in this imposing courtroom with twenty or thirty lawyers.

This sculpture in Derry is inscribed:

Doire le Duchas
Ag Gaelu Dhoire
Bilingualising Derry
Bi Broduit As Do Theranga
Be Proud of Your Native Language
Labhair Gaeilge

It reminds me of the work being done in New Zealand to acknowledge and preserve te reo, the Maori language.

We read that two boys have been suspended from school because their parents are refusing to let them go to the compulsory Irish language lessons, saying the subject is irrelevant and the boys are not to learn it. But Ireland is the best place to learn and speak Irish, just as New Zealand is the best place in the world to learn and speak Maori.

And in Galway, parents at a two-teacher school have withdrawn the entire roll of twelve pupils because a travelling community wanted their nine children to begin school there. The other parents felt this would dominate school life for their children. The travelling community has moved on, saying they would prefer their children to go to a school where they were welcome.

Tonight Jack has gone to film the Buncrana Bridge by the Doherty Keep, which is floodlit at night. He is also going to spend time at the Grianán of Aileach and will lie under the moonlight in the middle of the huge ring fort that was of such significance to his ancestors… I hope he returns!

My stolen and shamed blood-red hand

New Ulster asks who am I
Old Ulster lets me know

My ancient giant's blood-red hand is
Stolen and shamed
Yet flies on flags within my home

It terrorises my young school-bound daughters
The world and I watch
Not understanding, many weep
I have seen the splinter in my enemy's eye

A travelling family's children
Are refused entry to school
They are grubby and on the move

Their travelling sin — the sin of difference
Our settled sin — the sin of indifference
For peace's sake
How long before we bear
Or dare
To celebrate our differences?

Maybe too long
How much the cost?
The cost of our own bloodstained hands

Jack Doherty

*New Ulster was an early name for part of New Zealand

Donegal Dolmen.

9

A New Job and 9/11

I have at last been offered a job in Dublin. Having an income means we will stay in Ireland and not catch the plane home with Alice in three weeks, but living in Dublin was not in our plans at all. Although I have adjusted already, I know Jack will find it harder to leave Donegal behind.

The position is that of chief officer for the Council for Children's Hospitals Care. Dublin has three hospitals for children, and this joint council was established to co-ordinate and integrate them to help improve paediatric services. The council has seventeen members from the three hospitals and the health funding board, as well as the chairperson, Dr Helen Burke.

The council is currently reviewing paediatric surgery, exploring ways to reduce the ear, nose and throat surgery waiting lists, and will soon review information-gathering systems and unnecessary admissions of children to the hospitals. Developing strategies that improve accessibility and equity, as well as the quality of the services provided, is an important role of the council.

I find an instant rapport during the interview with Helen Burke. She is most interested in my Union Health Service experience and the way that a community development model of health service, placed alongside the medical model, can change health outcomes. I am excited about the position and the council's efforts to improve the health of children in the greater Dublin area, including Wicklow and Kildare.

There are only three on the staff — Helen, myself and Marian, who provides administration support. The council also contracts a consultant for specific project work. I report to Helen. This warm, friendly woman who already feels so familiar to me has phoned to discuss the position and the next steps. After farewelling Alice on the plane to New Zealand we will have lunch at her home, which I suspect will be a much-needed distraction.

"We'll put the men out the back and have a good talk about community development and such matters," Helen says. "Please Holy God we'll have plenty of hours to talk in the future. I've been desperately worried you might not take the position. After working alongside those grand Maori people in New Zealand, I hope you realise you have to swap all that for tricky hospital consultants?" When I explain that I will always remember who the service improvement is targeting, Helen says, "My own starting point is those who are most often overlooked, so we're off to a grand start."

She adds, "Now, Jewarne. The position is thirty-three hours a week and you being a married woman like myself, not to mention the desprit Dublin traffic… We are very flexible, so you just turn up when you can get there." I laugh, wondering if it will be my duties as a married woman or the Dublin traffic that will make me late for work. There is an Irish solution to everything, and I am so looking forward to working with Helen Burke. The referee checks are all favourable, and I have accepted the position, much to her relief. She can now sleep at nights!

A walk along Rathmullen beach gives us time to think about farewelling Alice, how to tell our Donegal family we are moving to Dublin to work, and to plan how to make the most of our last three weeks together in Donegal. It's blowing a gale, and it feels like the strong wind is just what I need to turn my life in this new direction. As we head into the wind, I look up, expecting to see Jack's brother Paul

A decade in between

There was a decade in between us
The day that we first met
We laughed and warmed together
The Doherty boys were set!

You looked brown and friendly
Mothering four blonde girls
I was young and shy
In love, amidst the whirls

The walks along the beach began
That summer of '73
One of the treasures we've always shared
Solving problems by the sea

We laughed and cried and wondered
With Kapiti in the fore
Leaving the beach with answers
Gathered on the shore

Our children have loved each other
The brothers make sure of that
The cousins connect with each other
There's plenty of noise and craic

There's a decade in between us
You've always led the way
As your footprints stay on Kapiti
Mine walk on Dublin Bay

When I turn 50 you're 60
New generations come out to play
We'll walk that beach next summer
It just might take all day

and his wife, Jan. We have enjoyed long walk and serious talks with them along Paraparaumu Beach many times over the years. I had written this poem for Jan's sixtieth birthday; she is more of a sister than a sister-in-law to me.

We end up at Portnoo beach on our way to see Donegal's biggest dolmen. These huge stones balanced on each other are humbling when you stand beside them and ponder their origin and purpose. The ancient in Ireland often stops me in my tracks.

All the letters from New Zealand comment on daffodils or freesias, and when I am in Dublin for the interview our niece Liz and our friend Sarah meet us by Molly Malone armed with a bunch of cream freesias with lime-green stems. Although it is autumn, in Europe you can buy almost any flower all year round. We eat together at a Mongolian restaurant where you select all your own stir-fry ingredients and spices, which they cook in front of you on an enormous wok. The food is delicious as we farewell Liz, exchanging her mobile phone for a book on Inishowen, and acknowledging all the special times we have shared with this niece of ours in Ireland.

On 11 September we are horrified by the film footage from New York. Alice calls me and we watch most of it live while our friends and family in New Zealand are sleeping. Suddenly it is scary to be in Europe, and the urge to head back to the South Pacific is strong. Three text messages arrive within hours. Jude writes: "George W is having kittens — hold on Earth!" Jec sends one from Sydney asking, "Mum is this World War Three starting?" My sister Claire's message simply reads, "Come home now!"

Jack is at a three-day aquaculture conference in Letterkenny at the time of the attacks. He comes home later in the day and our trio is vulnerable, lonely and a long way from New Zealand.

There are hundreds of Irish firemen and police in New York, and about 44 million people identify themselves as Irish Americans. Ireland has a national day of mourning with schools, workplaces and even pubs closing for the day. In Letterkenny the firemen meet for a memorial service, and a leather baffle on the cathedral bells makes them ring more dully and deeper than usual.

Margaret and Tommy's son John lives in New York and they wait to hear from him, but the phone and internet lines are blocked. Alice is due to fly out in ten days via Los Angeles, so we will follow developments closely. We receive nine TV channels here, and yesterday eight of them had the news coverage. The American channels focus on distressing personal stories, whereas the British channels air more analytical discussions or debate about the events. One commentator says the choice is now technology versus theology.

But right now, for the first time in twenty-four hours, not one channel covers the story. A bomb has gone off in Derry with no injuries reported, so I have turned the TV off and the house is peaceful and quiet.

Over the weekend the Kiwis I know in Ireland come to Letterkenny to celebrate my birthday. More important, we also gather to keep each other company when we yearn to head home because of world events. The Devlins and Sarah come up from Dublin, and another Sarah arrives from Scotland. Alice enjoys the young company, and the girls' chatter and laughter fills the house again.

They stay at home while we tour ancient sites on Saturday, but on Sunday we all walk up the river from the Doherty Keep in Buncrana, picking blackberries and a vivid bunch of pink and purple heather and thistle flowers. We stop for a latte in Derry and a drunk man asks if we are all sisters. This is an unexpected birthday gift for me, sitting beside the two 22-year-old Sarahs.

We have a drink at McCafferty's pub at the top of the hill above Letterkenny before returning home for a delicious dinner. The girls make a surprise orange and green birthday cake decorated with clementine and kiwifruit slices and two red candles found in the top kitchen cupboard. I have always loved my birthday in September in New Zealand because it's spring and new life with freesias, blossom and daffodils all around. I am displaced this year as the leaves turn golden and the supermarkets are beginning to sell bulbs to plant.

Before 9/11 we would notice the vapour trails of jets flying across the top of Ireland en route to America and elsewhere, white streams like the strips of Venetian blinds. This week with almost all flights cancelled, there have been no trails of white cloud in the Donegal skies. Alice is still positive and determined to fly home next week, though flights across America have only just resumed. Teresa, her primary school teacher and friend, will meet her at Heathrow, the first of many guardian angels who will be with her until she is home.

An article offers tips to worried air travellers and another is for parents wanting to help their children process what has happened. A full-page photo of a heavily armed soldier at Los Angeles airport catches us off guard. Air New Zealand has advised that check-in is now extended to three hours, and that hand luggage is not to include pocket knives, scissors, nail files or knitting needles. At LA Alice will now collect her baggage and clear Customs again instead of the baggage remaining in transit. It will be a long thirty hours before we hear she is safely in Hannah's arms at Wellington airport. "Text me immediately" will be the instructions sent with this precious cargo.

Any sadness about missing her will be minor compared with the pain of watching her trying to cope with living and schooling in Letterkenny. She will relish living with her big brother and sister and their families, as she was only eight when Josh left home to go to university and nine when Hannah did the same. Although she seems quite calm and confident about her trip, Alice has asked me not to ask her again how she is feeling about it.

Before we say our goodbyes we go over to Enniskillen in Fermanagh. It's an breathtakingly clear day, ideal to catch the ferry to Devenish Island. Maguire's Castle stands proudly on the shores of Lough Erne in Enniskillen. The castle was built by Hugh Maguire, but today the English flag flies there. Enniskillen is the town where the Fenian uncle of our friends Jim and Don Matheson was hanged.

On the ferry we meet a Canadian man who taught in Masterton in the late 1960s. He is tracing the history of his great-grandfather, who was murdered by the IRA. No doubt the history of the castle, the flags that have flown above it and these two men's deaths are all interconnected. The new Bill Clinton Peace Centre in Enniskillen was the venue for a memorial service last week for those who died in the Twin Towers.

Devenish Island, County Fermanagh.

Devenish Island was the burial ground for the Doherty family's parish until the late 1880s when fourteen mourners drowned crossing the lough to a funeral. Since then parishioners have been buried on the mainland. We walk up the rise to the ancient graves with their indecipherable Celtic writing on the headstones. The abbey ruins sit beside one of the tallest ring towers in Ireland. It is moving for Alice, Jack and me to be here in this place, thinking of Doherty ancestors who either lie buried here or have visited to farewell others they loved.

On the way home we visit the Wright farmhouse in Killideas, near Irvinestown, stopping for a cup of tea with Mary and Stewart who live there now. Around 1880 the two Protestant Wright children married two Catholic Dohertys — which caused a scandal. Catherine Doherty had been looking after the sick Mrs Wright and Edward Doherty worked on the Wright farm. The two Wright children had been schooled in France and were well off compared to the working-class Doherty siblings.

There was tension in the district about the marriages, and when the Wright family were at the dedication of the new Protestant church their stables were burned and their prize-winning stud horses destroyed. We saw the charred windowsills and stepped over the blackened door frames of the old stables.

The two couples left for New Zealand to settle in Taranaki. Travelling with them was Bernard Doherty, the sixteen-year-old 'baby' of the Doherty family and Jack's grandfather. Stewart and Mary are restoring the house to its original state, and are interested in any old photographs of the house the New Zealand families may have.

Meanwhile on the internet I have started flat-hunting in Dublin. There are several agencies and after I type in the number of bedrooms, the suburb and the rent, I push a button and all those that match my wish list appear. After looking at the Dublin city map for several confusing minutes, I email or phone the key contact person. Our rent will double, but we will exchange the rental car for buses to compensate. The process of moving to Dublin, finding a place to live and beginning a new job is overwhelming but also exciting, with an inevitability about it. It feels right.

Kiwi update, September

My sister Kate has sent a beautiful birthday card showing Wairarapa daffodils. It is a print of a painting by Helena, who was Jessica and Alice's kindergarten teacher and a gifted counsellor, painter and doll-maker, and also a creative gardener. It sits beside my sister Gid's card of a little fairy in purple and glitter sending me warm wishes.

Lynette, a dear friend, has sent a card with news of Caitlin's birthday and Luke and Nuala's radio programme. My youngest sister Pip's long, newsy letter suggests that Hannah's nickname ('Bin') be used discreetly from now on, thanks to Osama Bin Laden. Jude is having time out with stitches in his knee after practising his snowboarding on a trampoline. Alice reminds us of the time he leapt in the air in the kitchen while practising his snowboard moves and cut his head! He and Josh are playing their first game of cricket for the season at the weekend, on opposing teams, at the Greytown Cricket Club. Roze follows up with a text saying, "Doherty bowled Doherty: 0: First ball", which would have given one brother (Jude) immense pleasure.

10

Farewell to Alice and Donegal

A whirlwind weekend in Dublin begins with a farewell for Alice at the Milano gourmet pizza restaurant with the two Sarahs and the Devlins. After dinner Alice and Joe Devlin go to a gig, while the rest of us walk along the Liffey to O'Shea's pub where nothing is happening. It's only 11 p.m. and people are coming in the door as we are about to leave. In typical Kiwi fashion, we are more than an hour early for all the craic.

We leave in various directions to catch buses. Emmett, Jack and I set out on the long walk back to the car. But Paddy Irish, a giant horse pulling a tiny cart, stops beside us. With a nod we accept his offer of a ride and sit in the cart amid Dublin's Friday night traffic and crowds. We clip-clop our way around Dublin's inner-city streets, stopping at traffic lights on the way to the carpark building.

On Saturday morning we are at the airport with Emmett, Tricia and Siobhan to farewell Alice. It's heartbreaking for everyone, until Alice decides to help us all by heading to the departure lounge early. Jack and I sit in the carpark and cry as our sturdiest tent peg waits by herself to fly home. It will be a long journey home for us too, made more apprehensive by the events of 9/11.

Alice has left us a note in the car.

Mum and Dad,
I can't thank you enough for a very special eight weeks!
I am lucky to have such wonderful parents.
I think what you are doing is great and I am so happy that you are doing it. I will be fine! Living with Hannah will be marvellous and I have lots of 'aunties' to look after me.
I love you both so much! I will miss you lots! Be Happy!
Enjoy! Make the Most of it! Love Each Other!
Eat something delicious! Wear your seat belt, Dad!
Love from your baby
Ali Rose xxxx

We sit in the car for a long time. I explain, as if I need to, that I am crying because I love her so much. Jack explains that he is crying because she loves him so much! It is difficult to imagine how our Irish experience will be without her, but we are soon to find out.

As Alice is flying to Heathrow, we manage to decipher the Dublin map sufficiently to arrive in time at Sandymount for the first of many meals with Helen and Kevin Burke. Helen's directions are tantalising and specific. "Now Jewarne, we are number six. It's a pale pink house with black railings and a rambling garden just two doors along from the statue of the naked woman outside the tax office!"

We find the naked lady leaning forward, throwing her arms in the air. I wonder if she has just paid a large tax bill, or has had news of an unexpected refund.

Kevin has prepared a lunch in the homely family kitchen just below footpath level. The view of the street's comings and goings and the front gate is perfect from here. After lunch Jack follows Helen's instructions for a walk to Dublin Bay, while Kevin attends to his regular afternoon 'project'. Helen and I begin to talk about work, quickly noting the many other interests and values in common. This is just the beginning of a long list of questions designed to discover more about each other and the families, communities and countries that have shaped us.

The work feels challenging and positive, and I am looking forward to beginning the chief officer position. Helen is hopeful that the work of the council will improve health services for Dublin children. She tells me the 'health media' are waiting to interview the New Zealander, which will happen on Helen's return from Greece. "Just mind yourself now, Jewarne, and read yourself into the position while I am away", she tells me.

Her welcome to Dublin gift to me is the authorised biography of Mary Robinson, which she co-authored with Olivia O'Leary. This is the highly readable story of a remarkable Irish woman who challenged both church and society as a human rights lawyer before becoming Ireland's first female president.

Helen and Kevin are to become our closest Irish friends. After three hours of their warm and generous hospitality, we leave Sandymount buoyed in spirit and ready to start looking for a flat. Meanwhile Alice is already flying across the Atlantic towards Los Angeles.

Sandymount is high on the list of suburbs in which we would like to live, but the rents in D4 (as this area is known) are high, and I would need to catch two buses or a train and a bus to work. The suburbs in the south have even numbers (D2, D4, D6), and those on the north side of the river are D1, D3 and D5. The lower numbers are closer to the city centre. I will soon come to understand why people give you a knowing nod if you mention someone living in D4, as this tree-lined area is one of 'the' addresses in Dublin.

We drive around Sandymount with the *Irish Times* on my knee. We decide to phone the very first advertisement for an apartment: "Luxury one-bedroom apartment, Bachelors Walk D1." D1 is north side, close to the inner-city and public transport. I ring Tommy O'Keeffe, the landlord. Tommy is having a viewing next week. I explain that we are here from Donegal for just one more day, so he sends his niece to show us the apartment. It's on the first floor and has the smallest bedroom ever, a bathroom and a lounge with a kitchen at the end. It looks over the Ha'penny Bridge and across the Liffey to Temple Bar, and is on Bachelors Walk just along from O'Connell Street. Both rooms have a balcon-ette with wrought-iron railings. The apartment has everything we need and Tommy agrees to change the couch for a sofa bed for our Kiwi visitors. He will make sure a new television and microwave arrive as we move from Donegal.

The Shoebox, Bachelors Walk.

The front door of the apartment is bright blue. It has the red door of the travel agent on one side and the purple door of the tanning shop on the other. The landlord's niece, Katie, is engaging and tells us not to worry about the apartment being so petite: "You just go to the pubs — there's millions of 'dem around here." The apartment building has an inner garden courtyard, "for sunbathing," the landlord tells me when he promotes the handy location. Nodding in my direction he says to Jack, "Herself can do the daytime shopping and the night time shopping and then there's always the all-night shopping as well when you live this close. You're handy to everyting here."

We quickly decide to take the apartment, astounded that the very first one we've viewed seems perfect. It becomes official. After almost thirty years of married life and five children, we will be moving in together in downtown Dublin. We don't even have to ask our mammies! This Shoebox apartment will be a project to concentrate on as we pack up our belongings in Donegal ready to move in.

In my pocket I have a timetable of where Alice is in the skies. For the next thirty hours I constantly take the scrap of paper out and check the time and position. I pray a lot of warm, calm thoughts for her as the plane goes from one coast of the USA to the other, and receive a variety of entertaining text messages from her siblings that keep me busy during her long journey home.

Hannah and Michael are celebrating their first wedding anniversary, revisiting Tauherenikau bush for a picnic: "Bubbly $7.99, strawberries and grapes. Singing tui is here again."

Jessica sends a distraction from Bondi Beach in Sydney: "33°. At hospital, torn stomach muscle surfing."

Josh sends a text from the train on his way to work in Wellington: "Enjoy being together with no kids. Where's Alice now?"

My friend Joan's brother Lew and his wife Jiff shifted to Ireland a year earlier, and live in flats overlooking Herbert Park. The ten-storey building, unusual for Dublin, provides stunning views both day and night. They invite us for a meal. It's great meeting other Kiwis here, hearing their experiences and listening to their advice about adjusting to Ireland. We leave their place soothed by the comforts of home cooking, and booked in for a quiz night run by the New Zealand Ireland Association during our first week in Dublin.

We stay with the Devlins and meet Sarah in the morning to drive south down the coast to Bray. Mrs Hanlon's B&B, where we stayed several years earlier with my sister Pip, still has purple and yellow pansies lining the front steps.

It's a glorious day through Dalkey and on to Wicklow and Glendalough. Sarah has brought a picnic, including a thermos of tea. Glendalough is a beautiful valley with two lakes. The remains of an ancient stone abbey are dwarfed by the Martello tower. We walk to the upper lake, around all the abbey sites, and sit on top of the hill at St Kevin's cell overlooking the lake. It is still with mirrored reflections, disturbed by the occasional fish jumping. There is a lot to pause and think about at the moment after such a momentous weekend, our time in Donegal ending and Dublin beginning. I can't think of a more peaceful setting in which to be still and to savour everything I am experiencing.

We return to Dublin over the Wicklow Gap and the lakes near Blessington to visit my cousin Christine and her four Irish daughters. We watch the

second half of the Gaelic football final with her. This game is huge over here, even bigger than rugby is in New Zealand. Galway win, and later that night in downtown Dublin a loud PA system plays 'The Fields of Athenry' — the Galway supporters song — most of the night.

Sister Loyola is seventy-six and is known as Bridie. She speaks on the radio about taking the miraculous medals of Mary to the team manager in 1998 to have them sewn on the boys' jerseys, and how they have been there ever since. I can't quite imagine the reaction to a venerable nun wandering into the All Blacks' training camp with miraculous medals and needle and thread in hand!

We hear a man interviewed about his dogs winning a championship at the greyhound races. When asked what helped them achieve this magnificent win he laughs quietly, admitting "Oh, all the rosaries and prayers were a great help, y'know — dat's for sure." The Irish seek and receive divine intervention for Gaelic football and dog racing and every other facet of life.

As we drive back to Donegal late that night the text message finally arrives from New Zealand. "Alice home in bed at Hannah's. Smooth flight. No armed men at LA. Nuala, Emily and Kate met her. Room all ready and decorated with her treasures."

Our last week in Donegal includes a visit to Portaferry, a quaint village an hour south of Belfast on the shores of Lough Stranford. While Jack meets with the aquaculturists, I study the Dublin map to become familiar with my new playground, and wait to have my hair cut at 'Snip & Snap'. Irish hairdressers have inventive names for their businesses, including one called 'Off Your Head'. Over the next few months I visit some that generously supply ashtrays for their customers.

The hairdresser tells me that the troubles in Belfast are only in pockets. There is nothing akin to it in Portaferry because who you are is never an issue. She also suggests quietly that peace will never happen in Belfast if the "small pockets" do not want it. When I told her we were moving to the centre of Dublin and I was concerned about the noise, she replied, "Ooh, I know what you mean — when I moved to Portaferry from three miles out in the country, it was terrible getting used to the noise."

A ten-minute ferry across the lough takes us to Stranford, and we drive home via Downpatrick and stop at St Patrick's grave. Northern Ireland is beautiful, including the two major cities of Derry and Belfast. I find it hard to choose a favourite place here. The Irish rarely refer to Northern Ireland and the Republic as separate places. There is a growing use of the terms 'Six Counties' and 'Island of Ireland', with the expectation that this land will one day be reunited.

Taking a day off packing, we discover Melmore Head, by Downings on the northern coastline of Donegal. The sand is almost white in the bay. Numerous caravans wedge together under the rock-faced hills. Summer holidays are over and the caravans look desolate. Some have decks, satellite dishes and garden sheds.

At the lookout over the dramatic coast we meet a friendly retired priest from Dublin. He used to come north to this wild Donegal spot and go fishing with his friend, a doctor. They had trouble getting the same day off. Two weeks earlier he had been asked to meet some Americans after 9/11. They were in Ireland for a golf holiday, and he took them south of Dublin to Glendalough. It was the perfect place, restful and spiritual. The Americans loved it, appreciating the Irish compassion and hospitality.

He leaned into our car window, saying, "Y'know, now, I couldn't resist getting my tuppence worth in. In the quiet of the chapel at Glendalough I said to the Americans, 'Maybe America needs to sit down and think hard about why on earth it has so many enemies'." His sentiments are common among the Irish I speak to.

When we finally arrive at Downings, the tweed shop that sells souvenirs is due to close for winter at Halloween and will reopen on St Patrick's Day. I am relieved I will be in Dublin over winter, as I suspect Donegal may be too quiet. But I will carry away many and varied impressions of the place. For example, it's struck me that monumental masonry is a busy industry here, and some memorials are large and elaborate Celtic crosses or statues. Florists must do well too; a hearse will often be covered in containers of vivid red or purple flowers spelling MUM, BRIDIE or even WIFE. Some of the graves are cultivated into beds of pansies, begonias or heathers in many shades of pink and mauve. The church also extends a remarkable degree of pastoral care to the living; at Jack's grandfather's church near Irvinestown a sign in the porch reads, "Attention Coeliacs — communion is available for coeliacs. Please notify the priest before Mass."

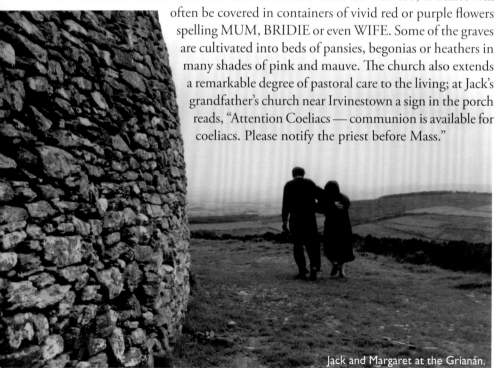

Jack and Margaret at the Grianán.

We revisit Derry for an interactive exhibition that takes us on a journey through history into the fifth province! Paddy Bogside has recommended it. The fifth province was once thought to be around Meath near the Hill of Tara, but there is a growing consensus that this is in fact the realm of the Celtic imagination.

When we first came to Letterkenny I was always conscious of going across the border into Northern Ireland. Now, eight weeks later, I pop over to Derry for the morning, feeling as much at home there as in Donegal.

Last night a journalist walking home from the pub in Armagh with his wife was shot by a Loyalist extremist group. John Reid, British Secretary to Northern Ireland, explains he was on the brink of declaring that the ceasefire was over, but decided not to when the Ulster Defence Party pledged they would ensure the end of violence. Now with this killing, the repercussions are unknown. It feels as if the extremists are showing their desperation. Peace and a negotiated relationship do not appear to be an option.

We spend our last day in Letterkenny with Margaret and Tommy Kelly. They welcomed us with open arms eight weeks ago and have made Letterkenny a memorable time for us to look back on. Margaret's sister Mary is buried beside her brothers, sisters, mammy and daddy at Killydonnel Abbey. We stayed with Mary eight years ago, and she sang a song for us about Enniskillen. The graves are just above the shores of Lough Swilly, beside the stone ruins of the abbey. We took Margaret on her first visit to the Grianán of Aileach, though she has lived along the road from the Grianán for eighty years.

At Mass that evening we pray beside this darling old couple who have welcomed us like their own children. It is a fitting end to our Donegal days. Earlier, Margaret said to me, "Mass is at 7.30 p.m. but Tommy and I always get there at 7 so we can say our prayers before Mass begins."

Donegal moods

for Jack

Will our bodies glow
Like the heather on Mount Errigal
And taste like the salt-driven plains
Of Tory Island?
So many shades of pink and purple
Reaching full bloom
In this late summer

Change comes abruptly
Sudden and sharp
Like the mist descending on Errigal
Grey and cold
Damp and frightening
I feel lost, cold
Alone

Is there an Errigal in Dublin?
Will Tommy and Margaret call?
Goodbye Donegal
I know you well
The Liffey flows in and out
We row the new currach
Strong enough already

Custom House
on the Liffey.

11

Dublin Views

Dublin is magic. After eight weeks in Donegal I am ready for its buzz and bustle.
Even Jack is adjusting quickly. Our Shoebox is at least warm and comfortable.
On our first day the sun bathes the rooms all afternoon and the moon shines on
the Liffey at night. Our view across the famous Ha'penny Bridge to Temple Bar
is only quiet from 4 a.m. onwards. At 5 the first trucks rumble along Bachelors
Walk on their way to the port, and the busy traffic follows. It all happens beneath
our window. From our first-floor living area I've made eye contact with commuters
on double-decker buses. It is disconcerting, but after a quick smile or a wave the
bus moves on towards O'Connell Street.

Emmett, Tricia and Siobhan are our first visitors. We break bread, drink wine
and light the candle they bring to place among the Irish rocks, the paua shell from
Aotearoa New Zealand and the acorns from the Doherty Keep in Buncrana. Derry
(or Doire) means oak grove. We bless the house with the water from the holy
well of Doon in Donegal and eat out together across the river in Temple Bar. The
shouting and laughing goes on almost all night. I wake often and have decided

to find my ear plugs, and am becoming used to the idea that it is not someone coming to visit us whenever I hear a noise.

Jack walks me to the bus stop on the first morning of work to catch the 123 bus. I pay 85p and ten minutes later arrive at the front doors of St James Hospital. Marian is beaming and delighted to have a colleague at last, and no doubt intrigued it is a New Zealander. The prefabricated building is dilapidated and surrounded by similar buildings used by the mental health workers. But my own work space, next to Marian's, is light and fresh with new furniture, a diary, laptop and a comprehensive map of Dublin. Marian takes me out for lunch and a tour of the hospital that includes a bank, chemist and post office. I spend the week reading myself in as Helen instructed, and setting up the files on the computer. Marian is grand, a real gas as they say here, capable and efficient. Everything I need is clearly accessible and well documented.

St James Hospital is between two notable Dublin sites. On one side is Kilmainham Jail, now closed as a prison but open for tourists to hear the tragic history contained within its walls. On the other side is the Guinness factory. Sometimes when I walk home the strong smell of brewing almost forces me onto a bus. It is a contrast to the predominance in Donegal of the sweet peat smoke in the air.

Part of my orientation is to visit the three children's hospitals and meet key people whose names I have read in council documents. The children's section in Tallaght Hospital is only four years old — and a long taxi ride from my office. Catherine and Maura meet me in the atrium of leafy trees in the centre of the hospital where people wait. A chamber orchestra and a mime artist have performed in the atrium recently. The children's wards and the designated paediatric spaces in the hospital, including Accident & Emergency, radiology and the short-term stay unit, are bright and friendly. Every space is designed with children in mind. Every bed has either a parent's bed beside it or there is a parent room at the end of the ward. My quick tour includes the laboratory, a familiar environment to me even thirty years after my laboratory technologist days at Wellington Hospital.

Temple Street Children's Hospital is close to the inner city, but a taxi ride here can take almost as long as the journey to Tallaght. The traffic can be "desprit", a versatile adjective used to describe both the traffic and the weather. Rita, the Director of Nursing, walks me up and down the narrow hallways and stairs of this old building. I feel as if I am visiting someone's home. Rita stops to talk to all the nurses, and is proud of their dedication and the services they provide to children and their families in the limited space. Designs and plans for a new hospital nearby have been approved.

Our Lady's Children's Hospital is in Crumlin, and the closest to my office base at St James Hospital. Emily, Director of Nursing, shows me the extensive network of wards and departments, all named after saints, as she explains the specialist paediatric cardiology service for which this hospital is renowned. Each hospital offers specialist services as well as more general medical care. Through the council these hospitals will work together more closely. I think I will enjoy the position and its challenges and in particular the people I will work alongside.

The walk home from work takes thirty minutes along the river in the sun. I begin by the Guinness factory and as a rule walk down to the Liffey by Christchurch Cathedral, passing billboards advertising Dublin concerts and gigs. The river looks dirty some days, the water thick and black. When the tide is out a slimy green rim appears along the stone wall, and it looks like a bathtub in need of a good clean.

Memorial behind Dublin Castle.

Sometimes I stay south of the river and wander through Christchurch, pass by Dublin Castle and walk through Temple Bar. At night the lights reflect on the river, especially the crimson lights from the pizza restaurant directly opposite our apartment. The bridges along the Liffey are all distinctive, so I walk across a new bridge each day. The weather has been mild and dry and people stroll the boardwalk at all hours of the night.

A few doors along from our apartment on Bachelors Walk are two places we become familiar with: the Church of the Blessed Sacrament and the Arlington pub. The church is a simply-designed place of prayer. When I close the heavy doors the noise and business of Dublin is shut out. I enter to light a candle for our friend Marie, who is giving her brother Michael a kidney in New Zealand today. The church notices include a recent travel raffle result.

1st Prize: Pilgrimage to Lourdes for Two: Ticket No 28678
2nd Prize: Pilgrimage to Fatima for One: Ticket No 02626
3rd Prize: Pilgrimage to Lourdes for One: Ticket No 12825
4th Prize: Pilgrimage to Medjugorje for One: Ticket No 23630
5th Prize: Mini cruise to France for Four: Ticket No 15359

By way of contrast, the Arlington is a huge, busy, noisy pub. Our local has a band playing every night with Irish dancers performing. It hums with crowds seven nights a week, singing along to all the favourites — 'Whisky in the Jar', 'Dirty

Old Town', 'The Fields of Athenry', 'The Leaving of Liverpool', and all the Celtic soccer songs. 'Flower of Scotland' always receives a raucous response from the many Scottish visitors to Dublin. My friends and family in New Zealand would love it, and I wish they were here.

Our team at the New Zealand Ireland Association quiz night is called 'John Mitchell's Spies' (after the current All Black coach) and Emmett, Jack, my cousin Christine and I come seventh out of seventeen. The venue is upstairs at Mother Redcaps Tavern. The winning team is 'Palmerston North Pies' and all the teams have adopted colloquial Kiwi names: Bugger, Dublin Anzacs, Jaffas, One-Eyed Cantabs and Kia Kaha. Prizes are bottles of New Zealand wine and pies. The pies are donated by a Kiwi man who has started a pie business in Dublin after being unable to find a decent pie to eat in Ireland. (We had to laugh once when we saw a 'Full Ulster Fry' pie for sale. It was full of bacon, eggs, tomatoes and black pudding.)

My visa expires in three weeks, so early one morning we head to Immigration at the local garda station and find several dozen people waiting in hot, cramped conditions. Many are sitting on the floor trying to appease hot, tired babies and children. Most are black or Asian, and few speak English as their first language. No interpreter service is provided and minimal information is available about the process and the steps to follow.

After a frustrating attempt to access information, I step into the 'Staff Only' section and find a worker who is able to tell me:
- I can't be seen without a ticket.
- Tickets for this particular day have run out so I won't be seen at all. (It is only 9.30 a.m.)
- Tickets are distributed at 8 a.m. and are limited to the number of people the staff can see in one day.
- When I do have a ticket I may be seen any time between 8 a.m. and 6 p.m.
- I must wait until I am called, and if I miss the call I will need to return another day.
- At 8 a.m. the queue may be onto the street, and around several blocks.
- I need to queue from 6 a.m. or earlier to have any chance of being seen, but there is no guarantee!

Despite being a confident, articulate English speaker I am overwhelmed and intimidated. I ask the woman why they don't have clear information available, and could they consider additional staffing. Her frank reply sums up the attitude I felt on arrival. "Well, we don't really want people to come in here!" As I leave she calls out across the crowded waiting area, "And don't forget you'll be needing to prove to us you're married when we see you."

When I arrive outside the Harcourt Square garda station at 5.30 a.m. the next Monday morning I am shocked but not surprised to see a queue already around the block into the next street. When I ask a man what time he arrived he says, "4.30 a.m. and look how far away I am!" It's freezing cold and drizzly, and these long queues are the same people waiting again, with children and babies. At 9 a.m. I am in the police station and receive ticket number 440. It is a long, cold day as we watch about twenty-five an hour being processed. Everyone waiting is compliant and powerless. Complaining may jeopardise a visa or residency application. The resentment and frustration is bouncing off the walls.

Just before 6 p.m., after almost twelve hours of waiting, ticket 440 is called. They take my photo and tell me I can stay for five years as I am married to an Irish national! (Later I will write a letter to the Police and Immigration about my experience, including suggestions for much-needed improvements.) On the way home I buy freesias to celebrate the end of a harrowing two days. My future in Ireland is secured for five years. I wonder how the others in the queue have fared.

In Dublin the footpaths are always crowded. When the rain comes extra room is required for all the umbrellas. I am aware of protecting my eyes and the occasional 'brolley rage' on the part of people in a hurry. Jack has planted daffodil, tulip and freesia bulbs in a box outside our lounge window. Underneath on the footpath, a busker is playing a tin whistle to entertain the people pouring off the Ha'penny Bridge. I am constantly surprised at the sounds and experiences of Ireland. I pinch myself and beam. This is Ireland and I am living here!

I have started reading Helen Burke and Olivia O'Leary's biography about Mary Robinson. I am only up to chapter six but I am finding it hugely enjoyable. This remarkable woman embarked on an enormous challenge when she tried to separate church law from civil and constitutional law, and promoted access to contraception and divorce as human rights choices for the women of Ireland. Mary herself is Catholic, and the negative reaction to her personally, and to her family and others supporting the cause, has been considerable. With 97% of the population of the republic Catholic, church and state in Ireland are a powerful combination.

I am struggling with my response to the beggars. I walk past children, youths, women and men who sit holding out a cup or a hand for money. They sit in all weathers on the Ha'penny Bridge, outside churches or in the doorways along Bachelors Walk. Although I have a pocketful of coins I am not convinced this will help. I see generous young Irish stopping to give money. Others visit discreetly late at night, stopping to crouch beside the homeless with sandwiches and a thermos of hot soup or tea.

At work last week a crying woman approached me in the grounds of St James Hospital. She is in a hostel with all her children but they have to be out on the street later that day. I have no money on me and mumble something inadequate like, "Do you have a community worker or social worker who can be alongside you and help?" Although I feel inept, she smiles and says "that's a good idea".

Back in Letterkenny, Romanian refugees approached me regularly on the footpath along the main street outside the post office, bank, supermarket or church doors. They shook money containers in my face and begged for cash. Many would hold their babies wrapped in blankets and block my path until I responded. I have heard the views of the locals and am aware of how my own response has changed since my first encounter. I am sure the Romanians have a their own story to tell.

The boys busking in Grafton Street earn their money singing, possibly under instructions from mammy to dirty their faces and sing off-key all day for the tourists. They have enormous buckets at their feet to collect the money. In time they get to know me and break into 'The Fields of Athenry' when they see me coming.

Along the quay from us, by the Customhouse, stand the Famine Statues, a graphic reminder of Ireland's past when many of our ancestors left their homeland. The sculptures are spotlit after dark, and they provoke my emotions whenever we pass.

Famine Statues beside the Liffey.

At the Offertory during Mass a collection is taken up, usually in open baskets, but in Dublin they collect the money in a bag with a zipper. My mother would never be able to take money out for change for our school lunches as she did once in our parish church, much to my horror and embarrassment when I was a stroppy teenager.

A woman near me in church taps my shoulder and cautions me to take my bag with me when I receive Communion, as it may not be there when I return. "Mind y'self now," she smiles.

An auction takes place every Sunday morning on the corner by the Dublin Woollen Mills across the road from our apartment. There are three or four vanloads of an eclectic range of goods for sale such as batteries, poached egg containers, biscuits, shampoo, umbrellas, teapots or toilet paper. Two classic items that make me laugh are the 'anti-tobacco smell' spray cans, two for a pound, and a Christmas tree for the car that plugs into the cigarette lighter and lights up.

This auction becomes Jack's regular Sunday morning expedition. The sellers are entertaining comedians with all the craic of Dublin. The buyers, mainly old men, some with bikes, huddle together in their jackets, long coats and caps. Hair curls from their ears, noses and eyebrows as they pull out pound coins from their pockets and secure this Sunday's bargain. My Sunday morning is spent at the café across the road from the auction reading numerous Irish papers and waiting for Jack to arrive for a latte with his bargain of the week. This week he heads off to buy an umbrella, but returns with a nativity set for the mantelpiece.

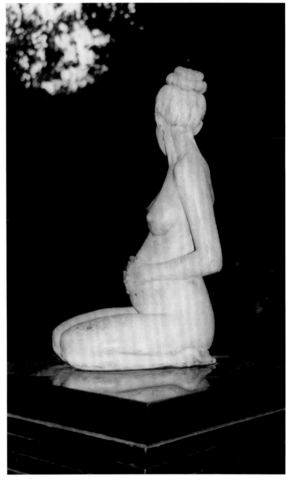

Merrion Square statue.

The Liffey 'wearing the nude' at low tide;
below, at high tide.

Anna Livia is the goddess of the Liffey. Ireland has twelve major river spirits, and their carved stone faces are on the Custom House building on the river. Anna Livia is the only female spirit. Ancient Celtic ritual included the offering of sacrifices by placing significant objects into special holy wells.

Jack wrote a litany of faces, places and images connected with Anna Livia. One night a Dublin reveller drowned just along from our apartment. His friends left messages and flowers along the boardwalk, creating a sad shrine that remained for a number of weeks.

Anna Livia Litany – *Jack Doherty*

Goddess called the river spirit	pray for us
Daughter of the Wicklow mountains	pray for us
Meander of County Kildare	pray for us
Guided by the glacial moraine	pray for us
Bridged by the ancient hurdles, Átha Cliath	pray for us
Shelter of the early raider	pray for us
Sustainer of the Viking town	pray for us
Divider of Dublin city, Duvh Linn	pray for us
Moat of the Norman Castle	pray for us
Container of patriot's spiked heads	pray for us
Gateway for the floating commerce	pray for us
Provider of the brewer's liquid	pray for us
Feeder of the great canals	pray for us
Holder of the enemy's gunboats	pray for us
Flooder of the Ringsend homes	pray for us
Taker of young drowned party souls	pray for us
Receiver of modern sacrificial offerings	pray for us
For ever and ever	Amen

Recent offerings to Anna Livia
found in the Liffey River.

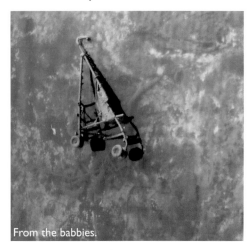

From the babbies.

Mammy's shopping.

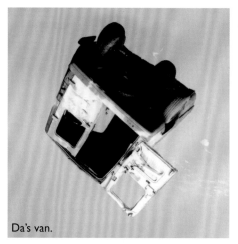

Da's van.

From the gossoons.

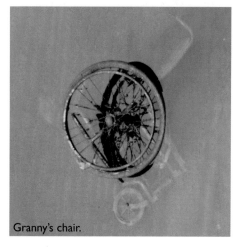

Granny's chair.

Kiwi update, October

News from New Zealand includes reports that our friends Peter, Pat and Roni have been elected to health boards and regional councils. Their values and skills make them ideal for these positions.

The leader of the National Party has been replaced.

Graham has sent a long report to Jack about Te Wakaiti, our community farm. His great love for the land shines out from every line.

Alice is starting work at Next Stop Earth, a flower and gift shop belonging to our friend Jeannie. Hannah's class has celebrated a netball win over Australia with a party at school.

Kath writes from her dairy farm saying Barney, our spaniel, has been the highlight of this year's Woodbury School pet day, coming second in a race and winning a chocolate bar. They are getting his red and black colours ready for the rugby football championship final.

12

REMEMBERING HISTORY

I am having a full Irish day experiencing both the pain and the joy that runs deep in this land. There is a gathering in the Garden of Remembrance for the men who died on hunger strike twenty years ago while seeking political prisoner status. They included a Kieran Doherty, the member of parliament for Cavan. I arrive outside the General Post Office in O'Connell Street — the scene of the 1916 uprising — to watch the parade. Thousands have gathered at the Garden of Remembrance and are marching to the GPO, led by the families of the men who died. The families walk beside each other carrying large black and white photos of their loved and remembered relatives.

There are hundreds and hundreds, of all ages. Marching amid the mass of uniforms, flags, drums, bands and banners are the H Block committees from throughout Ireland and Scotland, advocacy and support groups for the political prisoners. The procession takes an hour to go by me. I stand in tears, realising the cost of the past and the effort still required for this land to be free and independent. When Kieran Doherty's banner comes along I see Jack marching with the Dohertys.

The parade returns up O'Connell Street and stops at the GPO. A woman who has been a political prisoner presents her readings from a play about the women in Armagh Prison. Donal Lunney and a colleague play a lament. Another man plays a piece on the flute composed especially for the 20th anniversary. The list of the dead is read out, followed by the lowering of the flags and a minute's silence.

We go home for a Thai chicken curry with Emmett and Tricia, and later to our pub along the road for the Saturday night show. The pub is packed and a band has everyone singing. During their break dancers perform jigs and reels and the famous Riverdance sequence. Some riotous women from Scotland are in Dublin

H Block anniversary parade, O'Connell St, Dublin.

celebrating a 40th birthday, and when the band plays 'Flower of Scotland', the roof nearly comes off.

Another group of six arrive all wearing T-shirts that read *Happy 40th Birthday Peter, Dublin Tour 2001*. They are having fun and we find ourselves wishing once again that our friends and family were there to enjoy the craic, the Guinness and the Irish music and dancing.

H3 is a film about the political prisoners in the H Block leading up to and including 1981, when the hunger strikers died. The focus of this sad story is the men in prison and their relationships and brotherhood. Some scenes are quite violent. Emmett, Jack and I all cried; however, the film has been criticised for showing the prison guards in too good a light.

The Kiwis we know in Dublin are either our friends' children or friends of our own children. They are good ambassadors for New Zealand and for their families. When they come and visit us they all like looking at our 'Aotearoa Wall', which has many familiar, distinctively New Zealand cards and scenes on it.

Jessie, a friend's daughter from New Zealand, comes from Belfast for two days. She is our first overnight guest. Thomas the landlord has paid for a sofa bed, so our next visitors will be more comfortable than Jessie is with cushions on the floor.

Not long after, our friend Sarah returns from Portugal and I arrange to meet her and her friend, Louise, for a drink after work. I haven't been able to contact Jack for hours, and when I arrive home quite late I find him sitting on the stairs like a lost boy. He has been locked out since 10 a.m., with keys and phone numbers locked inside. He has heard the phone ringing constantly and by now is worried about what has happened to me! To fill in time he has seen a film and had a haircut.

Dublin is not like our home in Featherston where we didn't have to lock the house, or in Sunshine Bay where we can hide the key in a secret place outside.

Aotearoa Wall.

My job is going well. Staff meetings are held at Helen's home. She has returned from her holiday in Greece and the Council meets next week, so we are busy reviewing reports and documents beforehand. Helen will collect me tomorrow outside the Clarence Hotel — which is owned by U2 — as we are being interviewed by the Irish health media.

I have enrolled in a 'Med School For Managers' course for the next six months. Last week Helen and I went to a conference on the Irish health system held at the hospital at Tallaght. The theme was 'Confronting the Hard Issues' and it was a valuable introduction to the Irish health scene. Ireland is debating the same issues as New Zealand, with spiralling waiting lists and an emerging two-tiered system that can affect access to services for those with and those without health insurance. If you have insurance you get a date for the operation; if you don't, you get a place on the waiting list.

Those at the conference representing the travelling people, the homeless, mental health and drug addiction services, were emphatic about a third tier. They are advocates for those who don't receive an operation date or a place on the waiting list who just get nothing.

In Ireland, ensuring the consultants get paid comparably for their time is seen by many as a helpful solution. They receive a service fee for their private work and a salary for their public work. While there is meant to be a limit on the amount of private work they do, some consultants exceed the limit and some do no private work at all. Consequently the waiting lists grow.

A number of politicians are at the conference, including the Minister of Health, and it's good for them to hear the issues. The politicians are having their own debate about the options of funding health care through taxation or by compulsory insurance.

Primary health care in Ireland is markedly different from New Zealand. Many doctors still work without a practice nurse and many have no electronic practice management systems. The lack of community-based primary care networks means that people, especially children and the elderly, remain in hospital longer than necessary. There are limited home-based support services.

After our media interview, Helen and I make a policy decision to have lunch out together. She is great craic and we discuss all sorts of things, including the debates at the conference and her interest in New Zealand's health and social systems. I talk about her book on Mary Robinson and tell her about my children back in New Zealand who I am missing so much. She is keen for us to holiday sometime at the cottage in Schull, West Cork with her and Kevin.

The weather has been warm and dry all week. This is unusual and the city is in a spin. Everyone is talking about the weather. My new long raincoat, hat and red Dublin boots are awaiting the inevitable change to the 'desprit' weather more familiar to the Irish.

Today is the state funeral for Kevin Barry and nine other men executed by the British army after the 1916 uprising. They are being moved from the prison grounds to the consecrated burial ground in Glasnevin. I watch the lament outside the prison grounds and the formal Requiem Mass on TV at home, then join the throngs in O'Connell Street outside the GPO.

It is a formal, sombre procession of army, navy and air force personnel. Two soldiers fall out of line, fainting as they wait. The ten hearses arrive at a measured pace. Each coffin is draped with the Irish flag. Over 700 family members, politicians and the President follow them. When the first hearse goes past less than a metre from me, I look in and see the gold nameplate of Kevin Barry.

Kevin Barry was eighteen when he died, a gifted medical student, a good footballer and a hurling champion. Most of the men had not been convicted, only accused. They were all young, except for one who was thirty-nine and had ten children. Another had three children including baby twins, one of whom died in the mother's arms on the way home from the prison after the execution. The grief of the families is still raw eighty years later.

On the news tonight they interview a woman in her nineties who kept vigil

outside the prison gates with many other women, praying that the executions would not happen. Today outside the GPO an old woman told me the families have been lobbying for eighty years to have the men buried in consecrated ground. Others say it is the growing support for Sinn Féin and the upcoming general elections that have finally pressured the Fianna Fáil government to give these men the funeral they deserve and a proper burial in consecrated ground.

A series of programmes on TV feature Christy Moore and his guest list of singers and writers. They film the music and craic that happens. Christy is a wonderful singer and songwriter whom we have been privileged to see in New Zealand. There is also a new Monday night comedy *Bachelors Walk*, that was filmed on our street.

The seasons are changing. The prams of the women at the market in Moore Street are stocked full of Halloween goods. The crane on site at St James Hospital is covered in Christmas lights. The Dublin horizon is dotted with cranes on numerous building sites, and at Christmas they will all be decorated with lights and trees.

I always listen into conversations on the bus and watch the interactions. People on their mobile phones desperately try to say goodbye to each other, "Bye, bye, bye, bye bye," they say over and over. Also on the buses, young ones jump up instantly to offer their seat to anyone older. As the bus goes past any of the three churches en route to my work, I become aware of a movement through the bus, as (mainly) older people bless themselves. One morning at 8.30 three women board the bus in their ballgowns, their partners in tuxedos, all on their way home from a grand night out.

A couple of amusing Dublin dialogues take place after a taxi in which I am a passenger almost collides with a car. The taxi driver is going too fast, but the young woman driver of the other car has swerved into the bus and taxi lane in front of us with no indication. The taxi driver winds down the window and yells: "Y'know if you'd be wantin' to live a long life, you'd be needin' to give up droivin'!" The girls laugh and wave back at him. "They don't give a shite, y'know," he sighs.

He tells me that six years ago his Dublin house was worth £45,000 and today it is worth £260,000 thanks to the boom.

The same evening, we call in to a fish and chip restaurant and after our meal, order an apple tart. Your man says, pointing at the menu: "Yes dere it is definitely on the menu — but y'know, dere's none in the shop. You wouldn't believe it but foive people have asked for it today and do you know what? You won't believe it! We haven't had any apple tart in the shop since 1998!"

There is never a dull moment here. Every exchange is alive with an ironic or comic comment. I drink in every conversation and witty aside occasioned by sport, music, religion or just everyday life in Ireland.

After listening to an excellent band busking in Grafton Street we head to Doheny & Nesbitt's pub on Baggott Street with Emmett. Ireland is playing England in the final of the six nations rugby tournament. This game has been delayed several months because of the foot-and-mouth outbreak. Doheny & Nesbitts Pub is often featured on Irish calendars and postcards and is across the road from Baggot Inn — I used to think that Doheny was a spelling mistake for Doherty. It's a magnificent win for Ireland and the atmosphere in the pub is electric. You can't move for people, or hear, because of the resounding words of 'The Fields of Athenry'.

Another day Jack phones me at work with 'breaking news'. Several exciting options pass instantly through my mind, ranging from an end to the war on terror, one of my sisters arriving in Dublin, or just maybe Jack has found a job. The news is that the first daffodil shoot has appeared in our Dublin window box garden and he has taken the first garden photo. It's early, before winter has even really arrived, but it's a sign of hope and warmer days ahead — eventually.

Kiwi update, October

Yesterday I thought I could easily live here for years, but today I want to get on a plane and go home to celebrate Hannah and Patsy and Pip's birthdays. I'd look forward to Marie visiting with her wicker basket, spending time with my sister Maree while she's nursing in Wellington and meeting my new nephew Thomas. Mostly, I want to see for myself that our children are as grand as they say.

Claire and Joe have visited Barney our dog and sent us a photo of him draped in yellow and black Hurricanes rugby football colours, after they heard he had been led astray into wearing red and black. Jessica reports that she now works in gloves and mask for Australian Post because of the anthrax scare. She will arrive in Dublin early in the New Year after five days in London.

13

Buses, Language and Gigs

At the bus stop an old man asks me if the No. 79 goes near Christchurch, an inner-city part of Dublin. I explain that he is asking the wrong person, but that I do know the No. 123 goes that way because it's my bus. He says he is waiting for the same bus but none have come, so he's wondering about catching another. Then he looks at me and says: "Y'know, the buses in Dublin are just like bananas — they come in bunches. And see dat timetable dere — don't use dat to find out when the bus will come. It only tells you how late the bus will be."

I decided the best suburb to live in must be Ans Seirbhís, as most of the buses are heading there, but I later discover it means 'Not in service'.

However you travel around this city, it's a busy occupation following the billboards, even if you can't get to all the gigs they advertise.

We were excited for all of ten minutes last night planning a trip to Belfast on the train to a Van Morrison concert tomorrow night, until we realised it was fully booked. Donovan has a gig here in early December and we have booked for the *Artists Against Racism* concert that includes Christy Moore, Mary Black and Jack's favourite, Sinead O'Connor. To see so many great artists perform in a four-hour show will be brilliant, even if they only have twenty minutes each.

Lynn, Jack's Welsh friend from New Zealand, is coming to stay for the weekend. He is on his way from Wales to the Isle of Man. The new sofa bed has just arrived and although we have almost no room for it, visitors will now have somewhere more comfortable to sleep.

It is a long holiday weekend and Lynn's visit coincides with the Halloween fireworks display along the quay and 8000 Dublin marathon athletes running along Bachelors Walk under our window. Lynn and Jack stand on the two balconies urging them on, four minutes after the start. Walkers and strollers yell and yahoo back. Some shout that they are on a pub crawl. Over 4000 runners from the United States have entered, and the race begins with the disabled athletes in their chariots. We walk along the Liffey to watch and hear the Irish commentator welcoming the athletes to the finish line: "Good on you Shaun — well done now — ooh, you're nearly there — grand effort — come on now, then — look you've done it: under 2 hrs 40 mins 40 seconds — it's only 39 seconds on the clock."

The garda next to me hears on his radio that the four men who passed us in a close bunch have changed positions in the last thirty seconds of the race. The black man from South Africa has beaten the Belgian. Turning to me, the policeman yells:

"Oooh, yer mun there, the black fella, he ended up winning, he did!"

We walk all of inner-city Dublin with Lynn seeing the buskers, beggars and artists and photographing him beside Molly Malone, Oscar Wilde, James Joyce and Anna Livia. After the fireworks display for Halloween we stay on at Fitzsimon's Bar and nightclub with a group of wild women from Edinburgh who make me want to be with my sisters again. They introduce us to their imaginary dog, Sandy, and create general mayhem by placing a white cardboard priest collar on Jack so they can go to Confession.

The taxi driver who takes Lynn to the ferry is great craic. Jack, after Jamesons and Guinness all weekend, slips easily into the vernacular: "Were you in the marat'on today, then?"

"Ah, no," yer mun the taxi driver replies, "not loikely. Oi wouldn't even droive it!"

Most weeks I spend an hour or two in Eason's bookstore in O'Connell Street. It's only five minutes from home and has an extensive Irish section of both fiction and non-fiction. On my way there, just by the statue of Daniel O'Connell on the corner, is a newsstand. I notice a magazine, the *Phoenix*. On the front cover is a photograph of George Bush and Gerry Adams in conversation.

George: "So it's the end of Republican violence then?"

Gerry: "Well, in Ireland anyhow!"

I am intrigued about the publication and asked the woman, "What is the *Phoenix*?"

"One punt eighty, dear," she replies.

And I see in the *Irish Times* today an article about New Zealand trying to resurrect its health system from a market-led model and head towards a population-based health service. Health is a service, not a business. Ireland is being urged not to make the same mistake as New Zealand by delivering a health service using a profit-making business model. I am featured in the *Irish Medical Times* as the new chief officer of the Children's Hospitals Council, from New Zealand, including a head-and-shoulders coloured photo.

The Late, Late Show on Friday night television is an entertaining local show of topical interviews and performances by musicians. It is hosted by Pat Kenny, who took over this role from the famous Gay Byrne.

This altar in the Bed & Breakfast near Ballyvourney, complete with a jar of Lourdes water, guarantees a good night's sleep.

Last night Pat interviewed the parents of the Cassidy quins, born at the Rotunda maternity hospital. The quins are thriving but are still in hospital. They have been booked to appear on the show after Christmas.

On the same show Mary Black sang two songs from her new album. She has three teenagers and Pat asked Mary what they thought of their mum's music.

"Oh sure now they are very polite, y'know. They wouldn't say it was crup, even if they thought it was!" Mary talked of the dilemma of a working mum doing gigs and concerts around the world and how she'd had to miss the confirmation of one of the boys because she was in Sydney. She talked of the difficulty of concerts being planned two years in advance when you have no idea when the Confirmation Day is going to be that year.

In a Catholic country Confirmation Day is part of the culture and weaves its way into an interview or conversation in a natural way. My adult Catholicism is much more about culture than religion and at times my spirituality is another thing again. I wonder if it is the same here for many people. Their humour and earthiness may include their friendship with their God. The devotion at holy wells and ancient sacred sites is strong even today, and I find myself lighting candles for people I am thinking of.

Earlier in the year the 'remains' of St Therese of Lisieux toured Ireland. Margaret in Letterkenny gave us a card with a relic of the material that the remains were placed on when they were resting on the altar in St Eunan's Cathedral. The sacred and the human are so often interwoven.

Irish culture has its own colloquial language and it too is intermingled with threads of religion as well as humour and everyday life. Dublin adds its own specific dialect and sense of humour to the mix and I am an eager student, hanging on every word.

Today when Helen rings from West Cork I tell her the long-awaited new premises for the Council may not happen after all. "Please Holy God, Jewarne, it will happen! I will get himself, St Anthony, organised immediately. I owe him fifty quid for the last favour so I'll pay that now and get right on to this one. Do you know what the last favour was?" she asks me. "It was filling the chief officer's position with your good self, and he did a grand job for me then. I'll pay up my fifty quid and get straight on to him."

Marian and I work well together and we stop for soup at St James every lunch time. There is always entertaining conversation to share. Her mother-in-law is coming up to Dublin and Marian is getting ready. "Ooh Jewarne, do y'know what I mean? Jesus, I'll be having to do a mammy clean of the house before the weekend!"

Desprit! This is how it sounds, never 'desperate'. Rubbish has spilled out of a bag in the hospital carpark and as I walk past it, a woman going the other way raises an eyebrow and says, "Desprit!" It is often used to describe the weather, and Marian arrives at work most days exclaiming that "the traffic was desprit." Life itself can be desprit, I can feel desprit; the word sums up any situation fast.

Craic is another I have come to understand and use. "The craic was great", or "Great craic" describes a good time over the weekend, an exciting game of football or a family gathering. I hear the young people on their phones on the bus: "Hello, what's the craic?" or "Any craic?" meaning, what's the news? Or "Come to Dublin for the craic." "The craic was ninety" means ten out of ten for quality. Christy Moore sings a song about the craic being ninety on the Isle of Man.

Religious phrases are inserted at the beginning, end or anywhere in the middle of a sentence and may include Please Holy God; Holy God Almighty; Jesus; God Almighty; Jesus, Mary and Blessed St Joseph; or, as our cousin Margaret from Donegal says, "Oh Sacred Heart of Divinity!"

When Jack enquires about a position being advertised, the conversation ends with the employer saying: "Well, I'd love to receive your application, look forward to getting it, God bless now."

"God bless now" or "Safe home now" are common farewells, but my favourite is "Mind y'self now, Jewarne." As I leave a meeting, work or a friend's home, this particular term of endearment makes me feel protected and loved.

A common complaint heard on a Monday morning bus ride comes from teenagers on their mobile phones: "I am fecked — totally wrecked. The weekend was brutal." Or "The car is fecked — it won't start." Taxi drivers prefer the noun, announcing "He's a fecker" or "a gob-shite", or just "a shite". My report to Council needed "a few little fecky changes", so this flexible word can be noun, adjective or verb. Any use conveys meaning quickly and clearly.

A listener will mutter "Go on, go on, go on" through a long story, or "go 'way, go 'way, go 'way", all said in a variety of intonations, depending on whether your story is sad, exciting, tragic or desprit.

The last glorious autumn colours in St Stephen's Green are disappearing. It's been the best autumn weather in Dublin for decades. "Wasn't yesterday a scorcher? It reached 11 degrees, y'know," the taxi driver says to me on my way to Temple Street Children's Hospital.

We make the most of the weather, exploring suburbs close to Dublin. We catch the train north to Howth (pronounced Howt by the locals) and enjoy a long walk around the colourful village and along the piers in the cold north wind.

Another day we travel south by train to Greystones and walk back to Bray on the coastal walk around the hill, above the rocks and the sea. The walk is just under two hours and includes a lunch stop with Kathleen, who we've met on the track. Kathleen runs a B&B. We part after sharing lunch and stories of life and love. It

A quiet evening at Howth.

has been a close and deep connection at all levels, despite the time we've known each other — just an hour on this wild track above the Irish Sea.

And on weekdays between job applications and interviews, Jack explores every nook and cranny in Dublin and spends a day in a sheltered place on Dublin Bay watching the wading birds on an estuary.

Early on a quiet Sunday morning we walk with Sarah to Glasnevin Cemetery to see this historic place with its amazing and varied collection of Celtic crosses. It is the final resting place of many famous patriots, including Michael Collins and Daniel O'Connell, and also where Kevin Barry and the other nine were reburied after their state funeral earlier in the month. On this Sunday morning the Irish Graves Association, who advocated on behalf of the families to have the men buried here, are gathered to have their own ceremony of honour. We are piped in with the people and watch as they lay wreaths and recite poetry, say prayers and listen to an oration.

Sarah gives us a copy of James Joyce's short stories, *The Dubliners*. She says it will be good reading while we were living in Dublin and exploring this city.

Daylight saving has ended, and abruptly the days have become colder, wetter and darker. As Christmas approaches we are feeling more homesick, so we have booked concerts to look forward to. Most exciting for me is the opportunity to see the Pogues. They are performing in Dublin just before Christmas. Our tickets say "No crowd surfing" and "No moshing", so I have emailed the children to find out what moshing is so that I can behave at the concert.

I remember my old Uncle Jack buying a *Best of the Pogues* CD and feeling very pleased with himself. A couple of weeks later he gave it to me, saying, "Here! Can't understand a bloody word of this."

The Three Nualas concert is hilarious; they review sacred Irish themes with humour and song, including the church, the bachelors and the politicians. It is advertised as their final concert, and earlier in the week an interviewer has asked them why: "Have you all fallen out, is there heaps of tension, is this why you're breaking up then?" he enquires. "Ooh no, no way, there's no tension or anything nasty — well, nothing at all that a good cup of hot tea can't help fix — in the face!"

Chris Kavanagh, a singer backed by excellent musicians, presents the *Tribute to Luke Kelly* concert singing many of Luke's famous songs. Luke was a songwriter — known as the King of Balladeers and a member of the Dubliners — who died of cancer in his forties.

African woman in Dublin

African woman in Dublin
Your beautiful hair is hidden
By a short straight shiny wig
Being yourself here is forbidden

African woman in Dublin
Your belly swollen with child
Robed in colourful garments
You have nothing at all to hide

African woman in Dublin
The bus door slams in your face
Your bags and your pram are full
The commuters need your place

African woman in Dublin
You've left so much behind
A hundred thousand welcomes
Is that what you had in mind?

The Modern Art Gallery in Dublin, which used to be the soldiers' infirmary, has a vast grey cobblestoned courtyard. Below the gallery, underground, is the Grass Roots Café, which sells the best café food I have tasted in Dublin, and Helen and I have lunch there one day. Another time, after a meeting at the Department of Health and Children, we eat in an Irish-speaking café nestled under the footpath. I say thank you in Irish — the words are displayed by the till: "Go raibh maith agat."

Tomorrow night we are invited to Helen and Kevin's home for 'kitchen-dins' and will meet their daughters Katie and Sara. Helen tells me 'kitchen-dins' is when we eat together in the kitchen as a family would, instead of in the formal dining area. It sounds ideal, and we feel included in their family.

Kiwi update, November

My sister Maree is going to Sydney where she will meet Jessica, and she promises to send me a detailed "mother report". Jessica writes advising us that moshing is something to do with all moving together in the 'pit' at a concert, so we are fully informed! Many comments have been received about the *Irish Medical Times* article, especially from my friend Patsy commenting on my facelift! (After media training here in Dublin, Helen and I wrote the article and submitted it as a press statement.)

Josh sends us a full report on the new All Black team, which arrives in Dublin in two weeks, and a ball-by-ball description of the Greytown cricket team game. Jude played as a special visitor in his op-shop cricket gear — a complete set for about $5. Josh says he ran around fielding with his long blond hair looking like the mane of a lion. Alice and Hannah arrived to watch their Doherty brothers score three runs each and both drop a valuable catch. "It's early in the season," the brothers said!

Nuala emails to say Alice is very happy. They are lying on the grass in the sun and I try to remember the smell and warmth of New Zealand grass in summer.

Emily, Matthew and Jack.

14

ALL BLACKS AND VAN THE MAN

My nephew Matthew and his Welsh partner Emily have arrived for the New Zealand versus Ireland rugby match at Lansdowne Road. Jack has negotiated a free carpark for them with the neighbouring hostel manager, a rugby-mad South African. We spend the first evening at our local, the Arlington, enjoying the Irish stew and Guinness and the usual evening of traditional music and dancing.

Dublin is full of Kiwis as many have come over from London for the game. Matthew meets friends as we wander home, walking around the block through Temple Bar. Early the next morning, with silver fern tattoos on our faces and holding the silver fern flags high, we meet the Devlins and head to the Lansdowne Hotel before the game. Emily proudly wears an Irish badge, announcing that the Celts need to stick together.

People approach us, asking where they can get the silver fern tattoos. "Oh you needed to get your mammies to send them over!" we tell them. On the way to the park dozens of stalls sell Irish and New Zealand memorabilia, including scarves, hats and pins. The women from Moore Street market wheel their prams full of chocolate bars and fizzy drinks, shouting "Choc bars, two for a pooound!"

One man is selling strips of pinned black ribbon and plaited headbands made of black wool. *For A Charity*, his sign reads. We stop to have a look and ask what the charity is. "Well," yer mun says, "I'll be quite honest with you. I'm unemployed meself and the money is for the mammy and the wee ones!" Jack and Matthew give him a fiver and some coins.

As we walk along beside the two-storey brick houses we see a banner hanging from an upstairs window. Painted on the sheet in big, black letters is *Bring Back Buck*. Buck Shelford was dropped from the All Blacks several years previously and there has been a protracted national — and now it seems international — movement to reinstate him. In New Zealand one persistent supporter carries a *Bring Back Buck* banner to every march on Parliament in Wellington.

In the ground, we stand at the northern end in 'Jonah's corner', about five metres in from the touchline. It is close to the action. The weather is fine and mild but the ground is fully lit for the 2 p.m. kick-off. We stand for the game, leaning on a rail, just as I used to when I went to games at Athletic Park in Wellington when I was a girl. Singing the national anthem and watching the All Black haka is spine-tingling, as is hearing the Irish supporters singing. I join in both.

After years of watching rugby internationals on television and hearing Jack say how much he'd love to be there with the Kiwis one day, here we are.

The first half is exciting for the Irish. The All Blacks look scattered and unsure ('crup' as they say here). The nephew Matthew is looking distressed. He is unable to watch much of the game because he was at Twickenham when France unexpectedly beat New Zealand in the World Cup, and perhaps he thinks history is going to repeat itself.

The Irish supporters around us are delightful company. One old man talks throughout the game. "In the end, ye know, it all comes down to the numbers," he says. Another calls out to a green jersey on the field, "Come on, mun, you're as slow as a funeral!"

The second half is better. It feels as if the Irish are the winners, even if the final score does not agree! At the end of the game, the old man beside us shakes Jack's hand, thanking him for his company, saying: "It was grand watching the game with you. It's hard to come by such good company these days. You be careful now, tonight, going out with the blonde in the long black dress. She can lead you astray!" The blonde in the long dress is a glass of Guinness and, yes, leading him astray is what she does well.

The Irish are fantastic losers, and New Zealanders can learn from them. They congratulate us all night, wanting to chat about the team and the game and especially Jonah. Emily says the Welsh are the same after a big game. It is hard to tell from their behaviour if they have won or lost. What is more important is the partying that happens before, during and after the game. It had been a satisfying match for everyone to enjoy and the craic after the game is ninety.

"The blonde in the long black dress."

We squeeze into the Lansdowne Hotel. The barbecue area outside, where the band play, is jam-packed so it takes time to find Sarah and my cousin Christine as we have arranged. The Kiwi boys are performing the haka and organising lineout and scrum practices with the Irish lads. The post-match analysis goes on for hours. Emmett in particular discusses all eighty minutes of the game with every friendly, engaging Irish supporter. Dozens of them queue up for a chat.

After this epic weekend, we welcome our friend's daughter Emma Maguire for her two-day visit to Dublin. Together we go on the Literary Pub Crawl. Two actors take us around the Dublin pubs that famous writers drank in and perform the writer's works outside the doors. They were "Irish drinkers with a writing problem", they say.

We visit Maguires Hotel in Dublin near the O'Connell Street bridge. Maguires brew their own beer, and this multi-level building of magnificent woodwork has an atmosphere to match. Emma is pleased to see they have even spelt Maguire correctly! She is nursing in London and makes pertinent comparisons with nursing in New Zealand. The morale is higher in London, as is the commitment to staff development and ongoing training. Annual leave is almost double, and the wages compare reasonably well. However, it is a struggle to feed the twenty-five patients on the ward when they receive meals for only sixteen. Emma has found herself mashing the potatoes with more milk to make them go further, and when the linen supply has not been delivered the nurses have used pillowcases to dry the patients. She feels she is a lone voice advocating for improvements to the service on behalf of the patients. Her visit goes too quickly, but she leaves saying that being a Maguire in Dublin feels just right and she will return.

After saying goodbye to Emma we have breakfast with Eugene at the North Star Hotel across from Connolly Station. The pub shakes and rattles when a train goes by. Eugene is a priest who we first met Eugene when he was the chaplain on the QE2 when it came to Wellington.

The man at the desk, a Kieran Doherty, shows us the way to the dining room. "Well y'know, y'go roight up the stairs there, roight up dem and into the elevator, and down to minus two."

We find this confusing, but along comes a man heading in the same direction and Jack says, "Here's a man who looks like he knows what he's doing." The man stares hard, then says, "I've never been insulted like that before!" Eugene is quite a character, a genial man, and an analyst of the Catholic Church, so we enjoy our reunion with him before he leaves for Galway.

Jack's search for work presents many an adventure, and catching a bus to Blanchardstown to deliver a job application is an experience. He visits the Dublin bus office in O'Connell Street to find out which bus is the correct one. "Oh it's a tirty-eight you'd be takin' dere" was the authoritative reply. He walks down the street and along the quay to the No. 38 bus stop. When he boards and asks for his ticket, the driver says, "Oh no, dis bus goes nowhere near dere, you'd be needin' a tirty-nine." Another walk up the road and along comes the No. 39. After listening

Clothesline at the Down Under Bar.

to the same request the helpful, friendly driver says, "No, dis bus goes nowhere near dere, but sit down by me and I'll put you off as near as I possibly can. You'd be havin' quite a walk, if ye don't mind now."

Forty-five minutes later he is left at a roundabout and pointed in the direction of a barren motorway. He eventually flags down a taxi. This kind of thing can be amusing, romantic and 'Irish', until you need to achieve a practical outcome or follow a definite timeline — then it just frustrating!

When we want to watch sport featuring New Zealand teams we head to the Down Under Bar near the top of Grafton Street. It is usually full of Kiwis, Australians and South Africans watching cricket or rugby tests between each other's countries. The New Zealanders are easy to spot, with their bone carvings and pounamu pendants proudly around their necks. Above the bar, hundreds of bras, undies, boxers and g-strings are pegged on a line.

One morning we when we go into the bar at 11 there is foam on the steps outside. The previous night there had been a foam party at the bar, and now there's a warning sign: "You could get wet tonight — no Gucci clothes please."

Along the Liffey on the new boardwalk is a café across the river from the Clarence Hotel. I meet Jack there on my way home from work sometimes and the craic with yer mun Sean, who makes the coffee, is wonderful. "Oh I know you're there. I'll be busy for a bit. Tell me what you want and then I'll know what the order is too. Now sit yerselves down and use one of those rugs that I stay up all night knitting on the loom." The lattes arrive and he looks at me and winks, then says: "Yer mun's coffee there. It's so strong he'll be awake until Wednesday. Yer don't mind do ye?"

We ask him if he lives across the river in the penthouse on top of the Clarence. "No, no, no. Yer mun Bono, leases it from me," he laughs.

The conversation usually includes the All Blacks and Jonah Lomu. Sean enjoys the story of the Kiwi Brendan 'Chainsaw' Laney playing for Scotland after only six days in that country; they call him the Celtic Kiwi. And Sean calls the Liffey the River Insane.

"What are the Kiwi women like, then?" asks Sean. Jack tells him they would love his accent so much there'd be no need to worry about the meagre contents of his wallet. We ask about the Irish women.

"I'm still interviewin' to be quite honest. Anytime they ring, I say I'm available any time at all for an interview. I don't like the wealthy women — too much baggage, y'know — prefer them poor, even a nacker I'd prefer to a wealthy one." The word 'nacker' is often heard in Dublin, and is a derogatory term for the travelling people.

When other clients arrive we share the rugs and discuss the weather and Dublin and the gigs. A man from Limerick nods at Sean and says, "Ah the Dubs — they're always a step ahead of the rest of us."

"You'd never trip one of us up," says Sean.

The Limerick man says that once on his return from New York, he was driving to Limerick and counted seventy types of rain. "Seventy," he says, shaking his head in disbelief at the memory.

We are frequent visitors to Sean's coffee kiosk on the boardwalk. One weekend his daughter Molly is helping. She is six, with a head full of vivid red curls.

Sean becomes used to Jack's visits during the day when I am working. One day I am walking home along the river after work and Sean calls out: "Come here to me, Jewarne. I had the Taoiseach, himself, stop for a coffee earlier on. I couldn't believe it! There was himself in a suit and tie and all dressed up. I thought it was Bertie calling."

Bertie Ahern is the Irish prime minister, and the title in Gaelic is Taoiseach. Jack thought he would surprise Sean by calling in on his first day at work, dressed in a suit and tie.

It is always well worth while striking up a conversation with a Dubliner and seeing what magic is woven; I am never disappointed.

The Van Morrison concert is great. The band makes superb music with saxophones, trumpets, bass and rhythm guitars, drums and pianos. Van the Man himself is aloof from the audience, but a cool singer and an accomplished harmonica and sax player. He performs all my favourites, and it feels unreal in our front row seats in the Ambassador Theatre listening to the songs we play in the car all the time. The theatre is intimate, so we feel on the edge of the stage.

While we wait for the doors to open, a woman in the queue says it's her third attempt to get tickets to a Van Morrison concert in Dublin. She warns us there will be no craic as he will just turn up, sing his songs and leave, and depending on his mood, the concert might be short or go on for hours! She is right. There is no interaction but I think he's cool enough on his own, with his misshapen black suit, black hat and dark glasses and that voice, with a band able to maximise every sound in every song. It's a treat to be there even if I feel guilty when I think of our friend Stephen back in New Zealand, who has brought many of Van's songs alive for us. When he sings 'Have I Told You Lately That I Love You' I think of my friend Mary and her love of Van Morrison's music. Van's version of this song was played at Mary's funeral. 'Brown Eyed Girl' takes me directly to Alice and her friends, dancing on the deck at Sunshine Bay at our millennium party.

The major distraction at the concert, and somewhat better looking than Van the Man, is Pierce Brosnan — two seats along from us. He arrives wearing a funny tweed hat that he removes when the lights go off. During 'Brown Eyed Girl' his wife jumps up and dances. Jack is unable to peep out the corner of his eye with his head straight, and I catch him staring at Pierce several times. I have to tell him, just like a school teacher, to face the front.

Sitting so close to Pierce Brosnan makes the evening even more unreal, and I can't wait to send Sarah a text after the concert: "Van the Man was great but Pierce was just two seats away!" At 3 a.m. we are woken by the doorbell. Over the intercom Sarah is yelling, pretending to be a journalist. "Hello, it's Judy Bailey from One Network News, Television New Zealand. I understand there is a breaking story about Pierce Brosnan in Dublin, and I have McDonalds to eat. Can I please come up?" She has arrived to share the moment and stay the night on the sofa bed.

Jack meets an old lady at the GPO today as they stand looking at the Christmas crib. He begins by saying how special the nativity scene is. The lady is sad and says, "Ooh yes, but the young ones don't know their religion — ye see, it's far too early for baby Jesus to be in there!"

"Well," says Jack, "the world is changing, that's for sure."

"Do you tink we'll all be wit' him eventually?" she asks hesitantly.

"Oh yes, I'm sure we will," says Jack.

She smiles and says, "Well I'm not committing any 'mortals', and I'm trying my best. I am, I am, I am. Do you tink the good Lord could ask for anything else?"

We really appreciate our Kiwi friends in Dublin when we gather at Lew and Jiff's house in Herbert Park for dinner and discuss events, people and places of keen interest just to us. We are sad about the death of international yachtsman Peter Blake and can imagine the feeling in New Zealand about his life and senseless murder. There is almost no coverage in the media here. He is unknown to the Irish, whereas they all know Jonah Lomu the rugby player.

One of the guests, Chris, who is president of the New Zealand Ireland Association, is from Palmerston North and we laugh at how we can just say 'Palmie' and everyone knows what we mean. After an evening of spirited discussions and plenty of humour we walk home in the crisp air about 1.30 a.m., wandering down Raglan Road on an autumn night, just like the song.

At the Artists against Racism concert a comedian is talking about the women of Ireland struggling with the World Cup soccer next June. "They'll be comin' down the stairs at 4 a.m. and yer mun will be there watching Scotland play the Himalayans or some country he's never heard of … and they'll all be doing their novenas to Our Lady of Perpetual Soccer!" The country apparently will be in a state of frenzy, and already the Minister of Education has announced that the Leaving Certificate exam timetable may be altered to fit in with Ireland's matches in the World Cup.

Penny's department store is packed on a wet Saturday morning. The public address system blares: "We interrupt your shopping, customers, for an important announcement!" I am immediately alert, thinking it's an evacuation warning because of a bomb or fire. Instead, it's the World Cup soccer draw for Ireland.

Kiwi update, November

Jec has received her Irish visa. She emails: "Can't wait to come and play with you, Mum and Dad. See you in March." Hannah and Alice have been to Robbie Williams' concert in Wellington and Josh and Roze are finalising their trip to Europe, including Ireland. They will arrive soon after Jec. Dublin is holding an Impressionist exhibition just for Roze, an artist, that includes 69 paintings by Monet, Renoir, Van Gogh and Gauguin. Mars writes that her grandson Ethan James won the Melbourne Cup sweepstake and all winnings are going straight into Granny's Trip to Ireland fund.

I've been having an acute attack of homesickness, mainly over Alice. This is greatly alleviated by a long phone call to her and Hannah. Next morning the phone rings and amid much cackling and laughter, Alice and Marie are playing the flute and tin whistle. At first I think it's the 007 tune after them hearing about Pierce Brosnan, but instead it is 'The Fields of Athenry'.

15

LORD OF THE RINGS, CHRISTMAS AND THE POGUES

Dublin is a complex and contrary environment for us to live in for a year. There is much to absorb and thrive on, to be puzzled by and to cherish. Many of our stories provide contrasting views of this place.

We are free of evening meetings or house maintenance and gardening, and the size of the Shoebox makes the housework quick to finish. In the evenings we read or write, watch TV (often TG4, the Irish-speaking channel), or go along to the music and dancing at the Arlington. Before bed we wander around the block — over the Ha'penny Bridge, through Temple Bar and back along the boardwalk. There is always plenty to see and experience.

This evening I pass a man begging on the footpath on Bachelors Walk. He has a red jacket and has nodded off to sleep. A cup for money is at his feet. In his hands he holds a wet cardboard sign: *Sleeping Rough — Not On Drugs.*

The old man at the bus stop outside Trinity College in a long brown raincoat waits for people to catch the bus and throw their cigarette butts away. He quickly stoops to collect and pocket them.

An old woman with a pink scarf on her head and a fag in her mouth wanders along under the Moore Street stalls, stooping to pick up the odd onion or potato that has fallen onto the ground. Outside the Trade Union headquarters I pass three or four homeless men on mattresses, covered in blankets of cardboard. They wake when the workers arrive. The young Irish are quick to put their hands in their pockets to give money, often turning back if they have walked past too quickly.

Another contradictory Irish thread surfaces in a talk we hear at Trinity College organised by Sinn Féin. A Colombian human rights lawyer speaks about trying to negotiate a fair trial and due process for three Irish men detained. He makes a passionate plea, describing the prison conditions and corruption in the country. Over thirty-five human rights lawyers have been assassinated in the previous three years. In the audience are family members of the three Irish men. The meeting is conducted in English and Spanish, and is held in the lecture hall where Mary Robinson used to lecture, and her role as Human Rights Commissioner for the United Nations is highlighted at the meeting.

We are waiting to catch the train to Malahide and a man begins to discuss the sacking of Warren Gatland, the New Zealand coach of the Irish rugby team. He is appalled at how the Kiwi coach has been treated by "the blazers", as he calls the rugby union men. "It will feck the whole team after the way he has built them up! It is the best Irish team we've ever had."

Many on the trains or waiting at the station are reading novels, newspapers or magazines. This is a land of readers, of literary skill and expertise.

The Irish première of the first *Lord of the Rings* film is hosted by the New Zealand Ireland Association. It is a proud evening for us Kiwis, especially when we read Freya, Ben, Luke and Jarl's names in the credits — our children's friends in New Zealand. The Irish audience cheer when it begins and again at the end. All the Kiwis remain until the credits finish, then cheer again. Featherston, the village we lived in for twenty years, is highlighted on the poster of Middle Earth that is now on the lounge wall of the Shoebox. After the film we are able to sign a book of condolence for Peter Blake.

Next day in the mail comes a card of Lake Wanaka in snow from our friend Rosaleen. It's blue and white with a red and green Christmas tree on the shore, and the postage stamp on the envelope has a picture from *Lord of the Rings*. The film is receiving high profile in the media, one BBC announcer proclaiming, "New Zealand tourism — brace yourself!" Photos of us at the première appear on the New Zealand Ireland website (www.nzireland.com) which keeps us up to date with events hosted by the New Zealand Ireland Association.

I spend a weekend on call with the surgical registrar team at Beaumont Hospital. This is offered to students on the Med School for Managers course. I am keen to participate but arrive apprehensive. It is two days spent in scrubs in theatre, following the ward rounds, observing surgical consultations in A&E or ICU, and sleeping in the doctors' residence. As an observer in theatre I am told where to sit and stand and not to touch anything blue or green. When the surgeon calls I am allowed to step forward for a closer look. Aneurysm repairs, bypassing arteries, a kidney transplant, gall bladder and appendix removals are all part of the weekend's work, and I'm fascinated.

At the doctors' lounge on Saturday night we order Chinese takeaways. I am sitting there feeling very equal, but definitely in a minority of non-smokers, when they begin discussing what they were doing in 1973. One young doctor wasn't born, another was born that year and another took his first step. They look over to me. "Mmmm. 1973? I was married that year." Laughs all around.

The theatre checklist reviews essential information about patients, ensuring they are fasting, have signed the consent form and removed their jewellery and dentures. Number four on this list of seven essential items is 'Last Rites', and when I follow the ward rounds on Sunday morning Mass is being televised to the patients.

On the way home from the hospital the taxi driver asks me where I am from, and which particular part of New Zealand. When I tell him he says, "Ah look, doesn't mean a ting to me — I'm no good at geometry, y'know." I smile and say I am the same.

While I've been away for the weekend Jack has been to the Munster versus Leinster rugby final with Emmett, and has been flying kites on Dublin Bay with Lew and Jiff.

The budget has been announced recently. Everyone is apprehensive about the 'recession', as only 3% growth is predicted for the next year. They have announced a new health strategy and plan to spend £10 billion over the next ten years. Even with the booming economy Ireland has enjoyed, the children's hospitals I work with still rely on fundraising street appeals and the sale of Christmas cards.

Paddy Power, the Irish betting agency, has been taking bets on the budget. You could bet on how many minutes it would take Charlie McGreevy, the Minister of Finance, to read the budget. I think it was a record thirty-seven minutes. You could even bet on how many sips of water Charlie would take during the delivery.

"*Le gach dea-ghuí i gcomhair — Na Nollag is na h-athbhliana*" my December letter home begins, wishing everyone a happy Christmas and New Year. Christmas is huge over here. I must never complain about the hectic build-up in New Zealand again. The Ha'penny Bridge has reopened after being under cover for renovations for months. It looks simply stunning with renewed paintwork, wrought iron and masonry. The streets are crammed with people carrying numerous shopping bags. Sometimes the mammies are hidden and I see a collection of shopping bags walking past me in the street. Arnotts department store has a chamber orchestra playing Christmas carols amid the swarm of shoppers. Every second shop plays the Pogues singing 'Fairy Tale of New York', and the St Vincent de Paul collectors are everywhere. The Welsh/Irish male choir is performing in Grafton Street wearing red Santa hats. Henry Street and Grafton Street look spectacular adorned with Christmas decorations and lights. A 'live' crib at Mansion House has real animals, and on the Liffey outside our window is the tallest Christmas tree floating on a barge. It is a Nestlé chocolate tree — all the decorations are multi-coloured chocolates or lollies with lights in them that reflect in the water. The city looks and feels enchanted.

Helen and Kevin host Christmas drinks and we enjoy an evening meeting their friends and family. One friend, Imelda, has recently celebrated her 50th birthday in New Zealand, and Sam Hunt the New Zealand poet was a guest at the party and performed his work. We also know Imelda's cousin in New Zealand and other mutual friends. The globe is tiny, and the Irish Catholic network in New Zealand even smaller. I am to copy Imelda the tape that Marie has sent us for Christmas that includes many waiata, the haka, the song 'Taumarunui on the Main Trunk Line' and Sam Hunt reciting a couple of poems.

As one of the Pogues says to the audience when summing up the Christmas concert, "Brilliant, fooking brilliant." This concert, at The Point on the north side of the Liffey, is exhilarating. We are seated above the dance floor, above the surging crowd. I decide moshing does not appeal to me, as I like to feel my feet on the ground, but the crowd surfing looks fun. It reminds me of the photo of Jude in a New Zealand Sunday paper, crowd surfing at The Gathering, a music festival on Takaka Hill at the top of the South Island.

The crowd is good-natured and patient. They chant "Shay-No, Shay-No" for almost an hour until your man, Shane MacGowan, finally appears. He is dressed in a neat black suit. His short, gelled hair looks dishevelled and all night he juggles in his two hands his glass, cigarette, microphone and lighter. He joins the other seven band members, wandering onto the stage like a duck, grabbing the microphone and saying, "Sorry we're so fookin' late." The crowd roars its approval! The fans adore him and every favourite is sung, backed by brilliant music, giving new life to traditional Irish music. I have always had a preference for the Rolling Stones over the Beatles, which I think is why the Pogues raunchy 'in your face' approach to Irish music appeals to me so much.

The security guards make vain attempts to keep people on the ground, throwing plastic containers of water over the crowd when the heat becomes terrific. Many in the crowd wear red Santa hats with *Happy Christmas your arse — Shane MacGowan* printed on them. The Irish flag is thrown onto the stage several times by the audience and tied around the speakers and the microphones by the band members. It is quite a spectacle and I keep wishing my sister Pip and our friend Patrick were here to revel in it all, especially when 'Dirty Old Town' is played.

The encores come around several times, including the crowd's absolute favourite 'Fairytale of New York'. When Shane and the female vocalist waltz around the stage during the instrumental part, the crowd goes crazy. We presume this is the grand finale and stand to leave when the crowd erupts with a deafening roar. The Dubliners have joined the Pogues on stage to sing 'The Rocky Road to Dublin'. This incredible collection of Irish musicians sing 'The Parting Glass' and we leave The Point buzzing.

In some ways the crowd has had the Pogues eating out of its hands instead of the other way round. We have been roaring through all the songs. The craic has been ninety-nine!

Christmas Day at the beach.

Just before Christmas Jack is offered a senior human resources position with the Eastern Regional Health Authority (ERHA). This news comes more than six weeks after the interview. I have been quietly wondering how long it would take Ireland to implement the new health strategy. The ERHA covers Wicklow, Dublin and Kildare counties, with a combined population of one and a half million.

Jack's days of exploring all things Irish are limited now and I will need to stop humming my theme song for him: "Six long months I spent in Dublin, six long months doing nuttin' at all".

Even more alarming, I have just lost an excellent housewife. I have cooked only two meals since we arrived in Dublin!

We spend Christmas at Herbert Park, as Jiff and Lew are in Scotland and think we will enjoy the extra space. Their apartment on the tenth floor has 360° panoramic views over the park, Dublin Bay and the city. It is near Raglan Road and a twenty-five-minute walk to our inner-city Shoebox.

The Dublin streets are strangely quiet and empty as we walk to midnight Mass in George Street with Sarah and her friend Briony on Christmas Eve. Everyone has left to go 'home' for Christmas. Spending Christmas Day at the beach is a traditional Kiwi pastime, so on Christmas morning we walk to Sandymount Beach wrapped in jackets and hats. The weather is 'Baltic', and we come home to feast on Aran Island salmon and, later in the day, a roast lamb dinner.

Christmas feels weird, stress-free and freezing. We manage to enjoy long phone calls to our children in New Zealand who are basking in the sun, enjoying barbeques and cold drinks.

On St Stephen's Day snow falls on Herbert Park for fifteen minutes. New Year's Eve is quiet. Emmett, Tricia and Siobhan come for dinner

Sarah at Sandymount.

and at 11.30 we stroll around the park block in the heavy white frost and under a full moon. We are back home in time for midnight views of skyrockets exploding over Dublin city. The pond in the park has frozen over and we spend New Year's Day throwing blocks of ice across the pond and watching children chance their luck on the ice. The ducks coming in to land are funny to watch, doing the splits, slipping and sliding everywhere in their attempts to reach the bread thrown by the children.

The Euro

Their battlefields stand witness
They bled each other for centuries
Some blood not yet congealed
Yet they grasp at a single round of metal

Britannia stands aloof
She always does
She might be right

My pocket is ready
Bring on the euro

Jack Doherty

Ireland begins using the euro on the first day of the New Year, along with most other European member countries. Britain has resisted this move so far and continues with a confusing mixture of Scottish pounds, Northern Irish pounds and English pounds. When you travel in Europe now, the *bureau de change* queues are mainly filled with those with sterling in their pockets. The euro eases travel in Europe.

KIWI UPDATE, DECEMBER

We receive a wonderful surprise Christmas present from Hannah, Alice and Roze — a video of our friends and family, including Thomas the new nephew. Sarah comes around to watch all the Featherston connections, so we hire a video player overnight and watch the tape five times. The girls are concerned it will make us sad, but it is the best comedy we have watched for years!

I have forgotten how light and open-plan the housing is in New Zealand compared with Ireland, and in particular with the Shoebox we live in here. The indoor areas flowing to outdoor decks and the garden features look inviting on the video. Everyone is quick to point out their Dublin Bay and Bantry Bay roses, and on display at Jeannie's flower shop, Next Stop Earth, is a large bucket of Bells of Ireland. The dogs feature prominently, including Albie who is scared of the camera, poser Tom showing off the shaved area where his dermatitis has been, Kate's bichon frise Paris centre-stage as usual, Gypsy chasing the rooster at Murphys Line, Rosie looking as scruffy as ever under the clothesline, and the dogs at Te Wakaiti farmhouse welcoming the video production team.

One favourite scene is the interview with Jude at Greytown Park during a cricket match. Seeing the McPaddens and Dohertys and so many friends makes us realise we have *the* most amazing group of children, family and friends one could hope for, and we look forward to our return home.

There is a gathering over Christmas and New Year at Te Wakaiti to celebrate 25 years since the community bought the land on the edge of Featherston. Many stories will be recalled and memories relived.

Jessica emails that they are taking the sofa from the flat to Bondi Beach over Christmas and that the sunsets are spectacular, affected by the ash from the bush fires near Sydney. Hannah, Michael and Alice are picnicking on Rabbit Island near Nelson with the McPaddens and Dohertys, and Jude is surfing at Castlepoint. Josh and Roze are working, and waiting for their holiday in Europe in March.

Currach boys, Emmett and Jack.

16

A New Year Dawns

Early in the New Year we explore Connemara with Emmett and Tricia. Connemara is north-west of Galway, an amazing palette of greys, whites and pale greens scattered around the stones and rocks that push through the land around the lakes. It is dotted with white-washed cottages tucked under any sheltered contour the land can offer. I love its wildness and the way the donkeys stand so still in the cold wind, sure of their place in this landscape.

After seeing the Indian film *Monsoon Wedding* I realise that Ireland — its landscape and housing and raincoats — is all greys and greens. It is beautiful in itself, but other colours are absent here. Megan, the daughter of our friends Pip and Pat, has emailed from India describing rainbows of saris drying on the ground. And I like the noisy and chaotic film about a family gathering for a wedding, containing all sorts of stories within stories.

The next week, the lush green rolling hills and broad lakes of Fermanagh make a contrast to rugged Connemara. We stay with Eileen and Frank in Fermanagh after hearing the sad news of Father Barney Doherty's death in New Zealand. We go with the Cassidy cousins to Mass in the Doherty's grandparents' church in White Hill. The priest prays for Barney and mentions that this was his grandfather's church and the area native to his ancestors. The Irish cousins met Father Barney and Sister Una in New Zealand three years earlier, as well as Sister Marie-Gabrielle, another cousin. All three have since died. Our last glimpse of home was Barney in his wheelchair at the airport beaming and laughing and waving those big arms from side to side, farewelling us. He was a loved and respected member of our Doherty family.

Farewell Bernard SM

I kneel before the altar of St Molaise
Focus of your grandfather's parish church
The soft rain of Fermanagh falls
Like the gentle weeping of your family
I taste the salt of my own tears
May God welcome you

Your body awaits interment in Aotearoa
Irish cousins mourn your parting
You are deeply loved here
Although your footsteps never passed this way
I sense the pride of your unknown ancestors calling you
As I weep with the living here who knew of you

My prayers extend to your three great families
The people of Samoa, your adopted family
The priests of the Society of Mary, your spiritual family
The vast blood lines of the Doherty clan, your birth family
May all of us who grieve be comforted by the Mother of your God

I pray for your friends and relations that enjoyed your blest company
They learned from you, the teacher
They played rugby with you, the coach
They were disciplined by you, the master
They prayed with you, the priest
They sought God's forgiveness from you, the confessor
They laughed with you, the character
They were comforted by you, the sufferer

Wellington now loses a last and rarest gift —
An old priest loved by the young
Barney, your full and joyful life affected us all
You deserve your high place at His right hand
Go beloved cousin, and join your sister Una

Poem for Barney, by Jack

Connemara horse
and donkeys.

January in Dublin is bleak. I am the coldest I have ever been and no sign of spring is visible. The trees at St James Hospital are bare-limbed and the crows have been busy building twiggy nests in the branches. You see much more once the trees have shed their leaves in the northern hemisphere winter. They say this is Ireland's mildest winter for years and there are blue skies most days. Even though it seems cold to me, it is much warmer than it should be. And when we come back home at New Year the tanning shop downstairs has been closed for the holiday week and we use the heater for the first time. Now that the shop has reopened, our little 'hothouse' is warm again.

The sales have almost ended in the shops and there is room on the footpaths again. I am looking at a mountain of men's jerseys on a table and the Irish woman beside me starts chatting. "Aren't the men eejits?" she asks. "They're more interested in a pint than checking out a new jersey." I love this opportunity to interact, so we talk about the sales and Christmas shopping. Then she says, "I tink it's us who are the eejits — why should we bother if the men aren't?" I don't tell her, as it feels too complicated, that I am looking in the menswear department for a jersey for myself.

In the fitting rooms the other women are friendly and helpful. They nudge each other and point at me saying, "Gorgeous! Doesn't she look gorgeous in that now? Buy it now, go on, go on. Himself won't mind at all!"

It is almost First Communion season here. You can buy little Sinead or Maeve a designer dress for €1000. I watch the fuss and antics of the mammies and grandmammies in Arnotts, cajoling the girls into trying on dresses and veils. The matching gloves, panties, shoes, parasols, tiaras and handbags are equally important. Reluctant boys appear from dressing rooms looking awkward in three-piece suits with matching ties and dress jackets. From the bus window on my way to work, a First Communion shop has a sign in the window: *Layby Now For First Communion,* and *Interest Free Credit for First Communion Attire.* It's a big industry here and one of the many problems I have with religion as opposed to spirituality.

In contrast, the Irish government, as expected, has announced an initial €80 million compensation fund for victims of physical and sexual abuse in Irish schools and orphanages. The religious orders and the Catholic Church have provided millions of euros in cash and valuable property as their contribution, and money has been set aside for counselling and helping victims heal. The relationship between the church and its people is changing quickly. Some feel it has never been alongside the struggle for freedom here in any official, overt way and has hurt and alienated the nation further by the abuse of its children.

There is a growing interest in pre-Christian Celtic spirituality, and we see a documentary about St Brigid and the female trinity — the maiden, the mother and the crone. This impressive combination was part of Celtic spirituality before St Patrick arrived with the Trinity of God, the Father, Son and Holy Spirit.

We see an interview with Sinead O'Connor. She is asked about her spirituality and what particular phase she is in. Sinead explains that she is allowing the pagan to lead the Christian. The indigenous will guide the colonised, I think.

I have these same contradictory feelings about being Catholic myself. It is a strong cultural influence in our family, handed down by generations of McPaddens and Dohertys. After watching people on the bus bless themselves as we drive past Dublin churches I now find myself doing the same, and when I walk past the chapel on Bachelors Walk or Our Lady of Mt Carmel Church near Christchurch, I go into the quiet and lighting a candle for someone who is especially on my mind that week.

Jack is going to the Carmelite Church on 2 February for the St Blaise liturgy. St Blaise is the patron saint of throats, and he wants to go and say thank you for his cancer cure. Although I sometimes mock and critique the church, I also actively seek and embrace rituals or practices that are real, meaningful and right for me. The indigenous Celtic spirituality makes sense of who I am and where I have come from. It is essential to my being. At times it even feels impeded by my religion.

We experience the theatre of Dublin over the winter weeks. I thoroughly enjoy *Behan Himself* with Niall Toibin presenting a retrospective look at the works of Irish playwright Brendan Behan, weaving song and prose through the play. His reading of a short story *The Confirmation Jacket* is classic entertainment as he enters and leaves the set several times, to reappear amid the other actors.

Stones in Your Pockets is a more serious play about a film made in an Irish village, performed by two actors who play four or five roles each, but with no costume change. They are very funny but the play has a sad ending. We also go to *Good Mourning Mrs Brown*, a comedy about an Irish mammy presiding over grandad's funeral, Father Quinn's failing vocation, and a couple of other equally complicated family matters.

On the first clear day of January we walk the Wicklow Mountains with my cousin Christine. Black Hill has expansive views of the Blessington Lakes where Christine lives. The wind feels like iceblocks whipping my face. The soft grass around the bogs looks firm until you step on it. I manage to get bogged a couple of times.

Jack has been following the New Zealand cricket team on the laptop by accessing a silent live score update every 60 seconds. New Zealand has been doing well, with some close results, so even the silent commentary has been exciting as he waits and waits for each update.

Rob is a New Zealand friend married to Anne from Dublin. We visit them for dinner and to share an evening with their six children, including one-year-old baby Hannah. Gregory, the older boy, is mastering the art of running from one end of the paddock and back with his ball balanced on a hurling stick. It is a tonic being in the company of children again — and sitting in the room in which two of our friend Stephen's Wairarapa paintings hang. We have always had a lot of children around us and our Dublin life feels out of kilter without them. Jessica feels the same — she has been camping with a friend, Lynette and her children near Sydney, and emails to say, "Mum I loved being near kids again!"

An unusual package appears in the mail. Since we arrived in Ireland we have been aware of protests and rallies to raise awareness about Sellafield, the nuclear power plant in England just across the sea.

The Irish government has sent every household potassium iodate tablets as a 'National Emergency Plan for Nuclear Accidents'. Being proud of New Zealand's nuclear-free policy, I am far from reassured by the arrival of this free gift from the Department of Health and Children.

Meanwhile the situation in Northern Ireland, especially north Belfast, continues to distress the people there as well as those here in the south. I wake each morning reluctant to hear the latest. There are big rallies in the north against sectarian violence after a postman is shot dead because he was Catholic. Loyalist extremists say they will target Catholic teachers and other postal workers, but a few days later withdraw this threat, and so it goes on.

Joyce, the cleaner at work, arrives late today and says, "I'm spreading myself

If undelivered please return to:
P.O. Box 5537, Dublin 2.

Postas Íoctha	Baile Átha Cliath
L	CEADÚNAS 5241

WARNING: KEEP OUT OF REACH OF CHILDREN

POTASSIUM IODATE TABLETS
**THIS ENVELOPE CONTAINS A MEDICINAL PRODUCT
AND SHOULD ONLY BE OPENED BY AN ADULT.**

84914506   101
The Doherty Family
40 Bachelor's Walk Apartments
Dublin 1

254

**DEPARTMENT
OF HEALTH AND
CHILDREN**
AN ROINN
SLÁINTE AGUS LEANAÍ
http://www.doh.ie

**National Emergency Plan
for Nuclear Accidents**

Lo Call: 1890 44 33 22

very t'in this morning!" She is always good craic and this morning asks me how old I was when I married. When I tell her twenty, she says, "Ooh, me ma was still washing my neck when I was twenty."

Her husband works in the fashion industry and has just taken a collection from top Irish designers to London. We joke that he could redesign her cleaner's uniform, but she says, "He's desprit — he wouldn't know a decent frock if it came up and bit him." Joyce is intrigued that we "have run away from the five children" as she sees it, and every day asks, "How's the love nest?" Her Christmas gift to me was a 'seduction candle' for the 'love nest'. Most mornings she checks that it is still alight and working.

She tells me about a young person 'acting the maggot', a variation of acting the goat in New Zealand. Every day my list of Irish words and expressions grows.

We notice many visually impaired and disabled people in Dublin, often carrying their white sticks — maybe it is the fastest way to move through the crowds on O'Connell Bridge or up and down Grafton Street. At the bus stop a man in a motorised wheelchair lines up beside me. The driver lowers the bus hydraulically and releases a ramp to give the wheelchair easy access. However once he is on board, he finds a visually impaired person sitting in the space where the wheelchair should fit. He is often on my morning bus, and today his black labrador guide-dog sits quietly blocking the access for the wheelchair. Two young people jump up; one explains to the blind man what is happening and takes him further down the bus to a seat, while the other helps the man with the wheelchair. Another woman, who doesn't look well, refuses to move to make way for either of them. The driver explains to me that under the European Community rules it is compulsory for all buses to have a ramp and an empty space at the front for wheelchairs.

Two films are shown this week about Bloody Sunday. One, *Bloody Sunday*, is from the perspective of the Protestant lawyer who helped organise the civil rights march that day (played by James Nesbitt). The other, *Sunday*, is from the point of view of the young Catholic 'bogside' brothers.

Thirty years ago in Derry, civil rights meant internment without trial for up to six months, and one vote per property owned. The Protestant businessman who owned six properties had six votes and the Catholic family with six adults living in one house had only one vote between them. These are some of the reasons so many in Derry marched for civil rights that day. Both films show the slaughter of the 14 civilians by the British army. Some were shot in the back. More than 30,000 are expected in Derry for the 30th anniversary memorial march. The people are still awaiting justice and an apology from the British Government.

The six nations rugby tournament begins and the Welsh have invaded Dublin. The city is a mass of good-humoured supporters dressed in red, singing in the pubs and enjoying the hospitality of the city. The weather has been wet and stormy and the Liffey has burst its banks along the quay from us.

I leave work early and wait for an hour for a bus until a man comes along saying the flooding in the city is preventing the buses from coming to the hospital. An hour later I arrive home frozen and wet after wearing several puddles when passing traffic sends huge waves washing over my raincoat and boots. After a hot bath I wait at the window to watch the high tide at midnight.

TG4, the Gaelic television channel, makes fine documentaries. They film the culture and the people, especially the elderly, sensitively and beautifully. One night I see an engrossing story about an Irish basket-weaver from Galway visiting his fellow craftsman in Tibet so they can teach each other their crafts, and another about an Irish currach-maker visiting an Inuit canoe-maker.

My favourite interview is with two old men who have been champion currach rowers around the islands off Galway. Neither will blow his own trumpet but each extols the amazing strength and skill of the other. One lives on a small island. They ask his wife how they had met. She explains that she came across to the island for a ceilidh, and a month later she returned for another one. At the second dance he asked her, "Would you like to be buried with my people?"

"And that was it!" she says, smiling into the camera. The romantic Irish, I think, but at a deeper level I see it is indeed a special and serious offer.

Kiwi update, January

Josh and Roze ring with the news that our first wee grandchild is due in September! We cry and hug each other, and later walk along the road to the chapel and light a candle for the three of them. I feel as if people on the bus must be able to tell just by looking at my smile. All the new aunties and uncles are delighted as well as the dozens of great-uncles and aunties … A new family member, and a new generation begins.

Josh and Roze visit here in March; Jack thinks spending St Patrick's day in Dublin with his unborn first grandchild will be just grand. I've been thinking September 2002 is going to be significant because I will be 50, but I can't imagine a more special gift!

Alice has turned 17. We ring her in the morning when she is walking through the school gates and again in the evening when she and her friends Lucy, Emily, Nuala and Anna have just had a picnic and a swim in the lagoon at the park in Wellington city.

17

WAITANGI DAY AND ASH WEDNESDAY

Waitangi Day is New Zealand's day for remembering the signing of the Treaty of Waitangi between the indigenous Maori and representatives of the English Crown. Being in Dublin on 6 February is a novel experience. The Down Under pub is playing Kiwi music and selling hot pies, New Zealand beer and Cheezels. The clocks in the pub are set to New Zealand time and are labelled Auckland, Taranaki, Palmerston North and so on.

The New Zealand Ireland Association hosts a Waitangi Day dinner, held in the President's Room at the Lansdowne Rugby Club. The catering is by PieCo, a pie company owned by a Kiwi, and includes pavlova, imported New Zealand hokey-pokey ice-cream and lamingtons, which the Irish waitresses have never seen before. The pie man apologises to his absent mum that the pavs are not quite a 100% because although he managed to find kiwifruit, he had no success in finding passionfruit pulp. The tables are named Kereru, Kotuku, Kea and so on after New Zealand birds. On each table is wine from Hunter's vineyard in Marlborough.

A man from Waterford is to speak about the Treaty of Waitangi. He has taught at Tokoroa, but is unaware that treaty issues are contentious in New Zealand and hotly debated. Before he begins Jack suggests he needs to be aware of this. The Irishman begins by saying that Governor Hobson was from Waterford, and explains that there was extensive debate before the Treaty was signed, and that without any fighting or shots being fired, the Maori pledged allegiance to the British Crown. He continues in a patronising style about "the lovely Maori people being wonderful singers and dancers, and I think we even have a Maori here tonight in this room."

At this stage a man jumps up and calls out, "What a load of crap — we never, ever lost to you buggers! We never gave a thing up." He walks out. People in the audience, mainly Kiwis, are interjecting and telling the guest speaker to sit down and shut up as he doesn't know what he's talking about. One man, unhappy with the raucous behaviour, cautions, "Call out by all means, but watch your language!" The speaker goes into school teacher mode, saying "Listen! Listen! I'm losing you, I'm losing you. Come back now." He tries to continue talking through the interjections and yelling, but eventually peters out.

Jack speaks with the man who has walked out. He is from Ngati Porou, on the East Coast. His mum is from Papawai Marae in Greytown, and he has lived and played cricket in Featherston, so knows many of our friends. I suggest the NZ Ireland Association invite Moana Jackson or Robert Consedine to a Waitangi Day dinner to present an accurate historical and current view of Treaty of Waitangi issues. New Zealanders are slowly learning their country's true history and working out how to go forward by addressing mistakes made in the past when the settler government failed to honour its responsibilities outlined in the Treaty.

Our friend Lew Skinner, in a buzzy bee tie, rescues the evening with his clever quiz questions. "Which cricket team was beaten today by Northern Districts?" he asks, and the crowd roars as one: "Canterbury!" The feeling in the room lightens.

Helen and I travel to Cork for a health seminar. We spend five hours on the train talking, mainly about social policy in Ireland and New Zealand. Helen is interested to hear about the Waitangi Day dinner, so we discuss the Treaty and the impact of colonisation on Maori health, language, education and general well-being. Helen's warm and witty personality makes fine company on a long journey, and we never run out of topics to discuss.

The seminar is about clinical governance and quality in health care, placing the patient at the centre of any multi-disciplinary team of clinical and non-clinical health workers. I understand that the idea of empowering patients is a more recent concept in Ireland and therefore threatening to some. The same has happened in New Zealand, where some may say the pendulum has swung too far.

The train to Cork passes through countryside familiar to Helen from her childhood, and close to the village of Effin. She laughs, telling me how as children they would be asking their mother if they could be going to the Effin church, or the Effin school.

Cork is charming, with the river weaving through the city, but today it is raining heavily and visibility is limited. The Cork accent is the most difficult for me to understand. It sounds as if they are singing as they speak, and Helen tells me that the further west of Cork you travel, the stronger the accent becomes.

Late on the evening of our return to Dublin I have another memorable conversation, this time with a taxi driver. He is telling me about his three 'luds', in particular his 19 year old who has recently left for New York. "Y'know, I threw a packet of condoms in his suitcase. I didn't say a ting to him of course. I hope he knows what they are for, but I tink he moight. Do you?" This had to be Irish sex education at its most subtle.

The Moore Street market sells vegetables, and on Saturday it's blowing a gale as the women shout out to me, "Foive onions for a euro, love!" or "Ripe tomatoes, sweetheart!" I comment to one woman how windy it is and she says, "Perished!

We will all be perished today in this wind, perished."

Perished, and worse, is how I feel for several days after visiting Kilmainham Jail in Dublin — by the bitterness and the cold and despair. It is physical and emotional. Children were imprisoned for stealing bread, and so many who died for Ireland's freedom were executed in the prison grounds.

Our tour guide is an excellent teacher, a young Irish historian who reminds me of the students employed at Newgrange and other tourism sites. We spend a long time in the education display area. I am particularly interested in the women's stories and their suffering. Grace Gifford's marriage to Joseph Plunkett in May 1916, just hours before he was shot at dawn, made me cry for a long time.

We come home after the prison visit to meet Angelene and Claire, New Zealanders whose parents we know. After dinner we spend the evening once again at the Arlington pub. The talk this week is that Mohammed Ali has Irish ancestry going back to Ennis in County Clare — where our Consedine friends are from and close to where my great-grandmother Bridget Clune was born. We also hear from an Irish comedian talking of the growth of Irish theme pubs around the world: "You won't believe it! They're in Germany, Samoa, Sydney, everywhere. I have even heard of a couple that have been opened in Dublin. But then, we Irish are always the last to cotton on!"

Kilmainham Jail, Dublin, and its courtyard where executions took place.

Six daffodils now bloom on our windowsill, and the freesias and tulips look promising. In the gardens around the city the snowdrops have been quite alone and prominent, but now the purple, golden-yellow and blue crocuses are poking through the barren ground.

My sister Kate introduced me to crocuses. She would always grow a few treasured bulbs in a container for spring. The American writer May Sarton describes crocuses in her journals as the harbingers of spring, poking through the snow in her garden after she had waited all winter for them to appear. Spring is my favourite season in New Zealand, but already I can see the colours in this northern spring are more vivid without the bright sun to fade them. The gardening writer in the *Irish Times* responds to my email asking where I can see displays of bluebells in Dublin, and we discover them under the trees in the Botanical Gardens.

It is Ash Wednesday. We have a whole new experience of this day being in a Catholic country.

Grace Gifford's cell.

Jack notices a message on his computer screen advising all staff that ashes will be distributed at 2.30 p.m. in the chapel on the second floor. His meeting is later adjourned for a few minutes so they can attend. People everywhere have ashes on their foreheads! The water in Athenry is infected with e-coli after the floods last week, and the TV news shows children queuing for water with black crosses visible on their foreheads.

The next news item has ladies at bingo being interviewed about the back pay for their benefits received today. They too have black crosses on their foreheads! The Irish soccer team is playing Russia tonight in a friendly game leading up to the World Cup soccer, in front of 43,000 at Lansdowne Rd. The Russian coach is shown smoking furiously, and the Irish commentator says, "Well, he obviously doesn't know it's Ash Wednesday today!"

Half the people at Jack's work have given up smoking for Lent, and a woman in my building who doesn't believe in God or go to church, is giving up takeaway food. I don't know how life would be here if you didn't come from a Catholic culture. It is all very familiar to me, but the context makes it more normal or acceptable. I am giving up pancakes after going to Sarah's flat for a Shrove Tuesday pancake dinner last night. There were about 14 there, all in their 20s, and after listening to the Irish talk about Lent I am convinced that being Catholic for them is more a cultural than a religious expression.

Cardiff Castle.

We spend a weekend in Wales with my nephew Matthew, and Emily. We fly to Bristol and Matthew drives us to Droitwich to visit Jack's cousin Tony and his wife Jean. Their expansive Tudor home, built about 700 years ago from wooden beams that came off a ship, was part of Catherine of Aragon's dowry. We drive to Wales off the motorway through the countryside, to see places where Matthew has worked during the foot-and-mouth epidemic. Wales is not as green as Ireland. It is rural and often hilly, with compact towns where the houses appear stacked together. We enjoy ourselves in the city of Cardiff and see the dramatic red dragon everywhere, including the logo of a taxi company named dragon.com.

After an Italian meal we walk through town and into the Walkabout pub where Matthew works. This is a favourite meeting place for Australians and New Zealanders. A sign on the wall reads, "Go Hard or Go Home!" The main streets are buzzing, full of young people.

The next day we go sightseeing with Emily while Matthew goes to rugby. His game is played in sleet, rain, snow and eventually brilliant sun, so while we are pleased we haven't gone to watch the game minus our coats (left behind in Droitwich), his team won and we are disappointed to have missed seeing him score, convert his own try and kick the winning points from a penalty.

Cardiff Castle is enormous. My only castle experience had been with Josh and Jude's lego, and it's quite enchanting to explore this one. The daffodils are opening up everywhere and the red dragon flies from the topmost tower.

By the time we've climbed to the very top of the castle, we too are feeling the rain, hail, sleet and a few snowflakes. The new millennium stadium looks as if a giant spacecraft has landed almost on top of the castle. It is a curious architectural mix. In the gardens next to the castle are velvet carpets of white and dark-purple crocuses.

We have a few drinks at Mulligan's Irish bar where Tom Jones is played all night. Everyone is singing along and when the bar closes at 11 p.m. we go to a nightclub called Liquid where a friend of Emily's is working and welcomes us into the VIP lounge. The city is full — the Worthington Cup football final had just finished — so we share the lounge with the Cardiff football team. Before returning to Dublin we have lunch with Emily's family and do our best to persuade them to visit New Zealand.

Jec has arrived at last! She flies into Dublin airport with her white hair and huge smile the same day that the Scottish rugby supporters arrive in their kilts for the Ireland versus Scotland game. I have never seen so many thousands of metres of kilts in such an array of colours and patterns. Bagpipes are everywhere in Dublin this weekend, including a lone piper on the Ha'penny Bridge. As we wait in the arrivals area for Jec, one man strolls off the plane with a swinging kilt but no hand

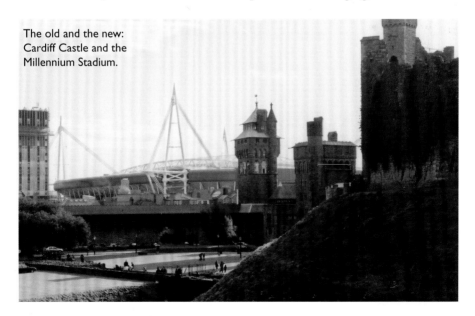

The old and the new: Cardiff Castle and the Millennium Stadium.

Spring in Cardiff.

luggage. Tucked into his socks is a tube of toothpaste and his toothbrush.

Snow falls in Dublin on Jec's first night, and we rush outside to take photos on the Ha'penny Bridge. We love her company. She left New Zealand to travel when she was only 18; now she's going to lead the quieter life with her parents while she searches for work. Weeks later we will still be pinching each other occasionally to ensure it's real. She cannot believe how deaf and visually impaired her parents have become since she last lived at home; she is continually having to turn down the TV or find a number in the telephone book for us.

When we come back from our planned trip to Scotland after Easter she will begin work.

Kiwi update, February

Josh and Roze are in Italy, heading towards Ireland. We have great reports from the Sevens rugby tournament in Wellington and the win for the Kiwis in cricket sounds good.

Recent New Zealand weather has been extreme. The weather here is very soft and mild in comparison, in spite of the Irish describing it as desprit, brutal and perishing.

Sunset at Slane Abbey.

18

A DOHERTY PILGRIMAGE AND ST PATRICK'S DAY

We are back at the airport again to meet Josh and Roze, who arrive from Edinburgh after four weeks in Europe. It is an emotional reunion — we all seem out of time and place. We head north in a new Alfa Romeo — after Jack gently nudges the new BMW behind us in the rental carpark at the airport. It is a beautiful day to show them Newgrange, after a picnic lunch with the new thermos, a packet of Krispie biscuits Hannah has sent and some Cadbury chocolate.

Newgrange is a dramatic introduction to Ireland for Josh and Roze as they stand in the narrow, ancient chamber where light enters on the day of the winter solstice. The passage tomb at Newgrange was rediscovered in 1699 when material was removed for road building, but major archaeological excavation of the site only began in 1962. We spend three hours at Newgrange. It's only an hour north of Dublin, and a compulsory stop for all our visitors.

We drive up the Boyne Valley to Slane and peep over the stone wall at Slane Castle where U2 performed. St Patrick lit his Easter Pascal fire on Slane Hill, challenging the high king of Ireland who lived on the Hill of Tara. The abbey ruins now sit on top of Slane Hill, and a climb up the internal staircase gives a view over the Boyne Valley.

The sun is setting through the monkey puzzle tree when we visit this time, and the hill of Tara is a silhouette in the background.

The apartment looks even smaller that night. The five of us talk long into the night, catching up on the news from home before we take our nightly stroll around the liveliest block in Dublin. Jec is keen to show Josh the bicycles abandoned in O'Connell Street. They remain padlocked to the bars, but many have no wheels

or handlebars. Her favourite has just its skeleton remaining.

As we drive north again next morning we tune in to Joe Duffy the talkback host interviewing Mary, a mother of ten who has just won the lottery. "Now tell us all about it then, Mary," Joe says.

"Well now, Joe," Mary begins, "I got the bus into town on the Friday, Joe. I was after havin' me hair done for the big 50th birthday party on the Saturday, Joe, and I was buying the ticket at the shop and havin' the cup of tea and sandwich in town before catching the bus home, y'know. Then there was the party and the next morning I was there reading the numbers in the paper and I was re-reading them a few times and then I was yelling out upstairs to the daughter. She was wearing the nude and had to get dressed first, Joe, and down she came and checked them and we got the son-in-law down the stairs to check them, and that night my sister came from Birmingham to celebrate and we had two bottles of bubbly left over from another wedding — or it might have been the nephew's 21st. Anyhow, Joe, we drank them."

When she stopped for breath, Joe asked her if she was seeking any financial advice or management, "Oooh Jesus Joe, there'll not be much left after the ten children and 43 grandchildren are looked after, and himself passed away — God bless him — 13 years ago."

Josh especially enjoyed his introduction to Irish talkback, and the expression 'wearing the nude' was often repeated on our holiday around Ireland.

We had met Tom McGuinness in Longford eight years earlier. Tom's mother was a Doherty and Jack's grandmother a McGuinness, so he marched Jack to the front of his shop as he yelled across the street, "Hey, Seamus and Michael! It's my fookin' cousin, all the way from New Zealand." Eight years on, Tom was jovial but quieter. His shop was overflowing with goods, the entrance almost impassable.

Jec at Slane Abbey ruins.

Pip at P. McPadden's, Drumkeerin

After a catch-up with Tom we headed towards Drumkeerin in Leitrim and stopped at the abbey cemetery on the shores of Lough Allen, where many McPaddens are buried. The P McPadden building in Drumkeerin has been demolished, so this photo taken of my sister Pip outside it eight years ago is a treasure now.

We find a lot of excuses to stop and enjoy places we travel through, like Carrick-on-Shannon, a quaint village and a favourite stopping place on Ireland's longest river for cruising boats and barges. In Fermanagh Jack leads Jessica, Josh and Roze proudly across the Doherty family land and shows them the views across to Devenish Island on Lough Erne, where many older generations of Dohertys are buried. We drive through Irvinestown and see the shop where Grandad worked before he left Ireland. It was Maguire's Drapery on our last visit, but is now Cheers Café, much to Josh's amusement.

Doherty Tower, Derry.

Later in the afternoon we amble around the walled city of Derry and visit the Doherty tower. The man at the desk says that if we have a few minutes to spare he'll find the keys and take us on a rare trip in the lift up the tower to the rooftop. The light in the lift is broken, so we huddle together in the dark, tiny box as we inch up four floors. On the roof, steps lead to the top of the tower and views over Derry from every angle.

Roze and I find wool and a pattern at Baldrick's wool shop in Derry so I can begin knitting for the baby. I can't wait to start. We drive over the border to Donegal, arriving at the Grianán of Aileach ring fort as the sun sets. The weather is fine but icy as we retrace the steps inside the ring fort that our other visitors have enjoyed with us. For Alice and her cousin Liz, and now Josh and Jec, reliving their Doherty clan history with a father and uncle passionate about the story makes them stand tall as Dohertys. Hannah and Jude will have the same experience in the future. By the time we arrive at the B&B across the road from McCafferty's pub we've seen Burt Castle and the key features of Letterkenny.

The next day is glorious. We eat a full Irish breakfast then leave to explore Inishowen, beginning with Buncrana and the Doherty Keep.

At the top of the steep, narrow lane leading to the Gap of Mamore, snow lies beside the road and the Donegal hills in the distance are white. We play with the donkeys in a field beside thatched cottages and one bites Jack's thumb, drawing blood. A nearby cottage has black wrought-iron gates with a harp and shamrock pattern and another, Rose Cottage is white with red trim and surrounded by a garden of daffodils.

We spend hours at Carrickbraghy, our favourite Doherty castle, picnicking in the sun and looking out to the Atlantic. Near Malin Head we stop at A. Doherty's pub for a drink, see Greencastle (of the Doherty clan) and return home to Letterkenny to meet the Kelly cousins.

We are at Ardara the next morning to introduce the family to Hugh and Philomena, but we find the shop empty. When Hugh eventually appears from out the back, he greets us with "Oh fook, it's you again then!" He lives up to my stories about him, running around the shop grabbing things to poke into our bags. Roze admires a turtle made of Donegal tweed and he shouts, "It's been here since the shop opened and sure ye can have it for free." When I inquire after Philomena he says, "Ooh now, mammy's in bed. She doesn't get up for winter. Why would you?"

After hot soup at Donegal town we drive south via Sligo and Knock to Galway and on to Doolin for the night. At Knock every gift shop is named after a saint. Vast amounts of Catholic memorabilia and sacramental objects are for sale. The modern church at Knock is huge and attractive with a lot of glass — unusual for Ireland. The carpark area is empty except for large black-and-white signs that read *Parking, Toilets* or *Confessions*. It's good to be there when it's quiet; I've been told it's a mini-Lourdes at times. Josh returns to the car shaking his head and describing Knock as a Catholic theme park. We drive on to see the sun go down on Galway Bay and the Aran Islands in an orange glow.

I sing the Clancy Brothers' version of 'Galway Bay' that I first heard in Wellington many years ago.

On her back she has tattooed the map of Ireland
And when she takes her bath on Saturdays
She rubs the Sunlight soap around by Claddagh
Just to watch the suds flow down by Galway Bay.

Josh wonders why fences are needed at all on the Burren as we drive for miles through fields of grey rock with no grass. We finally crawl into O'Connor's Farmhouse in Doolin for the night. We spend the evening in O'Connor's pub, by a roaring fire with two church pews either side. Coming in close to freezing, we sit down beside the fire but soon have to back off. Throughout the evening people arrive frozen, sit in the pew to thaw out, then make way for the next lot of chilled travellers. The music begins and we sit warm and happy to be together in the west of Ireland.

I love Doolin. It is known as the traditional music capital of Ireland. It is quaint and picturesque with about five pubs, a sprinkling of houses and gift shops and a couple of large hostels.

Early the next morning the Cliffs of Moher, Ireland's most visited tourist attraction, provide superb viewing. We are frozen, gasping at the dramatic views and the air temperature at the same time.

Back on the main road south, near the Consedine pub, is St Brigid's Well, an intriguing cave filled with statues and rosaries. We shelter from the rain inside the

Josh — How short were the Dohertys?

cave and wonder at the meaning of the human and divine mementos placed in this holy grotto. Of particular interest in one corner is a blue plastic Space Invader, resting on Mary's shoulder.

St Brigid's Well, County Clare.

It is a long drive home to Dublin through heavy rain, to arrive in time for the St Patrick's Day festivities. They begin with the Festival of Light on the Liffey outside our window. This is sponsored by the Allied Irish Bank and is called the 'Glimmer Festival', an ironic title given that millions of euros have recently been reported missing from this particular bank. The torrential rain means only a handful of the boats on the river are lit up. The bands of school children marching to drums and holding streamers and banners are saturated and look disappointed. The weather is desprit; the display on the river would be spectacular if the weather were better.

Fireworks the next night are equally disappointing. Thousands wait on the bridges up and down the Liffey, but the fireworks are set off down one end of the river around a corner, so people only see those that manage to reach the heavens. They immediately start to blame the government and are annoyed at the misleading advertising.

On Paddy's Day itself the parade through the centre of Dublin is the third event of the weekend. We join the crowds on the corner near our apartment and stand on the O'Connell Bridge. Rows of visiting American bands and other artists march and perform.

Is there cause, I wonder, for more celebration by the Irish diaspora on St Patrick's Day than for those who live in Ireland? The parade in Dublin is more subdued and not as much fun as those I have been to in Wellington. Others say the impact of 9/11 means the number of Americans visiting Dublin for the festival is greatly reduced this year.

A cottage in Doolin, County Clare.

Josh and Roze explore famous Dublin places, including the Guinness factory, which offers an excellent exhibition and tour. I particularly enjoy the history of their advertising and how it has developed over time, and the display of bottles used over the years.

Dublin Castle, the Book of Kells at Trinity, the Impressionist exhibition, galleries and nights at the Arlington are all fitted in before Roze and Josh fly home full of memories of their eleven days here. The next time we see them, their baby will be almost due.

We are in the groove of being Dubliners now, going to work each day and planning how to spend our weekends and time off. It is magic being here, and we are aware of how the weeks will fly. We have decided to return home in September. Our first grandchild will make this New Zealand spring a special time.

Cliffs of Moher, County Clare.

19

EASTER IN SCOTLAND

They are interviewing some Irish boys on TV about Easter. One says, "Well, what happened at Easter was that Jesus was very sad and worried so he went up the mountain to talk to his Da 'cause there were deese two tieves — one was a good one and the other a very bold one!" (The Irish use 'bold' to describe bad or particularly ghastly behaviour. It is quite a negative description. Some drunk men drove a crane off the Ha'penny Bridge into the river a few months ago, and Helen said 'the boldies' would have been responsible.)

As we leave Ireland on the Holy Thursday of Easter, Hannah phones to tell us she and Michael are having a baby in November. We were so happy for them, and surprised and overwhelmed to be coming home to two new grandbabies, eight weeks apart. We refer to this one as 'The Easter Egg' all weekend as we drive around Scotland, imagining what a change these babies will bring to our family.

We fall in love with Scotland. It is a land of mountains and water, rich with history and the Celtic spirit of the people. We drive more than 600 miles around the lochs, with snow on the hills and brown heather covering the land. They must be glorious in the summer in purple and pink flower. In the towns the bagpipes echo, and I think of our friends with Scottish ancestry in New Zealand and understand why I connect with them so well.

In Edinburgh we stay with Jack's cousin Brian on the Royal Mile, which runs from Holyrood Castle up the hill to Edinburgh Castle. Brian lives halfway up the mile. He spent three years in New Zealand and is a keen climber, mountaineer and snowboarder. At his place we are surrounded by maps of the Southern Alps, giving us a familiar environment to sleep in.

Brian's flat is on the fourth floor of a building that dates back to 1700. The circular stairwell up the side is a good test of fitness as we walk up to the door of the flat. After dinner we walk to Edinburgh Castle and enjoy the city late at night, ending up in the smallest pub in Scotland for a pint before bed. The room is tiny and a few musicians are having a practice session, playing the traditional Celtic music they perform at weddings and twenty-first birthdays.

A woman moves over to make room for me and we discover her New Zealand friend is married to the harbourmaster in Wellington, whose cousin I've worked with for the past four years. How many degrees of separation is that? The two women met in a maternity hospital in Edinburgh many years ago. The Scottish woman is now a granny, and tells me her new granddaughter, who lives near London, will be home in Edinburgh before she's two because they wanted her to grow up speaking with the right accent.

Friday morning is sunny as we head north towards Stirling Castle, where Liz has recommended a stop. Stirling Castle and the Wallace Monument are impressive, as is the delicious shortbread we discover on the way. Jessica is photographed outside the Church of the Holy Rude in Stirling, and we decide to drive on to Inverness, taking the smaller roads around Loch Earn and Loch Tay, lunching in the sun by the loch at Callin. The scenery is spectacular with the Highland 'coo' being the

Highland 'coo'.

Loch Tay.

main source of entertainment. Jec adores these hairy red cows and takes home a vast collection of Highland coo postcards, inside a Highland coo bag.

We drive along the lochs saying how we could be at Taupo, the Marlborough Sounds or the southern lakes of New Zealand … then around the next corner a magnificent grey stone castle reminds us that Scotland is quite different. We stop at the site of the battle of Culloden, near Inverness, where each clan represented in the uprising has a headstone in the fields. Fresh flowers and pieces of distinctive tartan lie beside the memorial stones. Sadness is in the air.

Memorial at Culloden.

Inverness is pretty, as are the villages along the way, and we stay at a B&B across the road from the river bank which is covered in daffodils. It is owned by a friendly Scottish couple who have Vegemite on the breakfast table just for Kiwi visitors. Ben Nevis is covered with snow as we drive south along Loch Ness to Fort William, and on to catch the ferry from Appin to Lismore.

Lismore is a long, narrow island with a population of about 170. We have a warm encounter over lunch with Tony and Cristall, who used to live at Western Lake near Featherston. Jack and Tony enjoy deep philosophical conversations, so the stroll around their ten acres includes earnest conversation, with arms waving and Tony's pipe puffing, while Cristall shows us the wild yellow primroses, the vegetable and raspberry gardens and all the trees they

Lismore philosophers.

have planted. Both are talented artists and we leave with a series of wildflower cards from Tony's originals and a map that includes prints of Tony's watercolours of the castles in the area.

Lismore is renowned for the variety and colour of the wildflowers in late summer, and Cristall explains how the spring flowers are courteous, taking turns at being on show. First to appear are the huge displays of white snowdrops, followed by the purple, white and gold crocuses. Then the daffodils perform, the primroses appear and, last of all, the vivid bluebells that she is waiting for. They have just returned from seeing their children and grandchildren in New Zealand. Their vitality always inspires us to live life as fully as possible. Tony drives the eight miles along the narrow road to and from the ferry, pointing out one of the island's three phone boxes and the primroses on the roadside.

Back on the mainland we drive further south to Ardrishaig village near Lochgilphead, the home of Julie, Jude's Scottish friend. Julie has sent us her parents' phone number and address with a message to "have fun with my parents". We are awkward for about ten seconds, as Blair and Susan have never met our son Jude and we've never met Julie. Their 1860 home is across the road from the loch and sits amid huge red and pink rhododendron bushes in flower. Deer occasionally wander into the garden.

We show them photos of the South Island and the Abel Tasman area which Julie is visiting at the same time we are at her home in Scotland. We stay at the Grey Gull Inn, and notice as we leave the sign in Ardrishaig: *Haste Ye Back*. (Speaking of signs, we have seen them in Ireland warning of wet floors: "Caution — slippy floor when wet", but in Scotland the same sign warns that the floor is skiddy, not slippy. There is plenty of material to entertain us.)

Waiting for the Lismore ferry.

On Easter Sunday we rise early and go to Kilmartin to the standing stones and ancient sites of the valley close to Ardrishaig. This part of Scotland has close links to the northern part of Ireland and includes the ancient kingdom of Dalriada, and Dunadd the seat of the kingdom. A woman walking in the misty rain tells us about the fairies and the dragon that protects the valley, and shares spine-tingling stories with us, so we visit the Kilmartin museum to read more history of the area before winding our way across to Inveraray and Glasgow and back to Edinburgh. Over four million of the five million Scots live in the urban band that includes Glasgow and Edinburgh, so it's as if the two cities almost meet.

We have 24 hours left to explore Edinburgh, so we walk up Arthur's Seat and look out over the city and its parks and out to the coast. It is hilly and inviting, with many familiar names to those who know Dunedin and southern parts of New Zealand. One of the pub menus offers 'Grandpa Crombies Auld Reekie Sausages', and Jack manages to find a feed of haggis and chips.

While we are in Edinburgh the Queen Mother dies and the flags are at half mast. On the Monday a forty-one gun salute is fired from Edinburgh Castle. This is a spectacle: the huge castle growing out of the rocks, overlooking an enormous bank of yellow daffodils and veiled in misty rain with the cannon firing.

A tour bus ride provides a brief history and stories of the city. The new museum is in Edinburgh stone, the peachy apricot colour that the rest of the city would be if dust, smoke and coal fumes hadn't discoloured it over the centuries.

Back in Dublin after Easter, Jec is working in the same building as the FM radio station. They ask if they can interview her; she'll be bound to win prizes. I find a radio at work and listen in as they say, "Ooh, that's not an Irish accent now is it?" They ask her about being a Kiwi in Dublin and living on Bachelors Walk so close to Temple Bar. She tells them, much to their amusement, that after being in Sydney she's looking for sun. She wins a box of chocolates, a T-shirt, a CD

Jack, one of the taller diaspora.

and tickets to a film, and is in the draw for a leather lounge suite. We would have trouble fitting that into the Shoebox. It's strange listening to Irish voices on the radio for months, then hearing this unmistakable Kiwi accent.

One night we go to JB Keane's play *The Matchmaker* with its masterful use and delivery of the rich and playful language of the Irish. It's witty, with two older actors, a man and a woman, both brilliant. One of the clients of the matchmaker has described himself as "an ex-jockey, seven stone, five foot feck-all, and likely to be missed in a crowd!"

The furore over the sexual abuse of children by Catholic priests continues. Several victims come forward together, demanding honesty from the church hierarchy, which is not forthcoming as they drag their feet and look incapable of responding. There is a strong push for all the church files to be given to the police. The Minister of Health has announced yet another inquiry. The question is whether it will be limited to one diocese, where victims and their families repeatedly but unsuccessfully requested that a priest be moved, or whether every diocese should be included. By the end of the week many other victims have come forward. One bishop has resigned, and this has caused a lot of anger because he will be absent for the inquiry into his negligence. One of the priests has since committed suicide. It has been reported that compensation to the victims of physical and sexual abuse may amount to more than €300 million.

The Irish seem ready for a mature and honest analysis of the role the church has played in determining their moral values, and the conflict at times between their preaching and practice. The role of the church will change for the future, and a demonstration is planned outside the Mass being held tomorrow for the Christian Brothers 200th anniversary of their founder.

It has been Jec's turn for a harrowing visit to the passport office at the garda station. Jack accompanies her at dawn with his Irish passport. They stamp her visa for four years because she is living with us. She's happy, and arrives home to tell me it will save her marrying an Irishman to stay here. Not that I'd mind an Irish son-in-law, I tell her.

Kiwi update, March

We receive sad news of people who have passed away in New Zealand, especially Michael's mum Sandra, who has died unexpectedly Also Olive Kelly, a regular visitor to Sunshine Bay, especially if there was a party on, and I remember her well at the millennium party dancing to the Irish music.

The Consedine's favourite 'aunt' has died in Auckland. One of them was always going to Auckland to see 'aunt', as she was always known to me. She died on her 88th birthday and was a wonderful mum and grandma to that family after their own died young. In the chapel along the road from our apartment, I light candles for them all, and for Kahu, a baby who has been abducted in New Zealand.

We talk longer than usual with Hannah and Michael, to celebrate the news of their pregnancy, then chat to 'Aunty' Alice, and 'Uncle' Jude, who is keen to hear of our time in Ardrishaig. Roze tells us they have been camping at the beach for Easter and the two new unborn cousins have met each other and had a good chat, tummy to tummy!

Jude emails to say that he jumped into the Buller Gorge, "the river of my ancestors". He has badly damaged the tendons in his knees and is in braces like Forrest Gump, he says. Alice has been to visit the Saywells and Barney our dog in Canterbury, en route to watch Ben in the rowing championships at Twizel.

Spoleto.

20

Italy and Pip

Jec is working for Microsoft in Dublin, and we have rearranged the Shoebox once again to create more space. I have been unsure how it would be, flatting with my twenty-year-old daughter who arrives home at 6 on Sunday mornings, but she is fun and we are enjoying the experience so far. Because Jec began travelling the world when she was only eighteen, we have lost time to make up.

Spring is slowly segueing into early summer, and the evenings are noticeably longer. At work I am busy finalising two reports that identify recommendations for implementation by the three paediatric hospitals.

Ireland is establishing a Public Health Alliance. A broad cross-section of health and community workers attend a meeting at the Royal College of Physicians. This Georgian building in central Dublin has magnificent ornate ceilings, and huge oil paintings of male physicians adorn the walls. The women's toilet is under the main floor, down in the dungeons. For many years, there was never a need to have one in the building.

A key paper is presented by a woman named Kathleen who works with women recovering from heroin addiction. Her talk highlights a community development view of public health and reminds me of the Healthcare Aotearoa network in New Zealand and the efforts to bring a community development perspective to health alongside the medical model. She begins by saying she is speaking for the women she works alongside who are too threatened and intimidated by the environment to speak for themselves. These women are poor, live in sub-standard housing, and are familiar with violence, poverty and extreme social exclusion.

But now the service is achieving positive results for them because the health care delivery comes from a community development perspective. The women's attempts to name their own health needs and access 'judgement-free' health care services are extraordinary, given the stigma they suffer as recovering addicts.

Kathleen identifies key areas of tension that health workers can expect to experience when a community development model is adopted, and I recognise them all from my own work in this area. Firstly, priorities chosen by the communities are often not the same as those chosen by the statutory agencies. Health issues as defined by local or national policies are often physical — for example, physical health problems, risk factors or low uptake of services. The community is more likely to have priorities that are social — for example, poor housing or limited childcare provision.

Also when people gain confidence and become more articulate through the process of community development, they are more likely to voice concern and criticism about the service, and this may threaten the health workers. There are no instant results and it takes time to know a community and build trust, whereas key reporting for projects often requires timely milestones and quick results. Authorities concerned about inequalities in health care may set up a project as a way of addressing the issue, but this is not the answer to complex and deeply-rooted causes of ill health like poverty and the colonisation of indigenous people. At best, the project may make a valuable contribution but, at worst, it can divert attention from the political solutions back to the problems.

I sit next to Kathleen at lunch and thank her for her presentation, which rang true for me. She tells me how nervous she was walking into the crowd of health professionals gathered in this vast room, its walls hung with oil paintings of male doctors. "Ooh Jewarne, I could feel my uterus contracting the minute I walked in there!"

In early summer Jack and I fly to Rome with Ryanair, arriving on a bright sunny morning. The first thing I notice is that my bones are warm, and I continue to enjoy that pleasure for the next ten days. I even need my sunglasses and a sunhat.

We are overawed by Rome. Our B&B is minutes from the station and quite central to the Colosseum, but we walk for miles up and down steps and hills, craning our necks at the buildings and alleyways and trying not to get run over by the crazy drivers who ignore red lights! In our first 24 hours in Rome we see four collisions.

I find Rome almost too much. If there were just a handful of statues, magnificent church ceilings or mosaic floors, I might appreciate it more.

The Italians have a profusion of pot plants, roof gardens and balcony gardens. Many of the photos I take are of a plaster wall with peeling paint surrounding a windowsill with red geraniums in a pot, or maybe a lace curtain with pansies in front of it. The urban environment is given life by gardens of the smallest size but most lavish colour.

The piazzas are a community meeting place. Our community is the tourists as we eat Italian meals at kerbside cafés, with the wine and music creating an unmistakeably Italian atmosphere. The Italian men gesticulate and debate and yell, waving their arms in every direction, and the women are exquisitely dressed with stilettos essential, worn with skirts, dresses, trousers and even shorts.

Rome is an especially revealing experience for me, coming from a Catholic culture. Although the art and the buildings are magnificent, the religious inspiration seems lacking; this is not the community-based church I am used to. I see nuns dressed in pre-Vatican II attire, like the Mercy nuns of my childhood. They are all in black with heavy veils and white bibs. Young curly-headed men stroll the streets as priests with their long black cassocks flowing. Shops sell vestments and monstrances, mitres and collars, and the back-to-front collar shirts priests wear. We see a shop window full of nuns' shoes and clothes, all in beige or fawn or navy, with no bright colours in sight.

A defining moment occurs for me when we arrive at the church of Saints Cosmos and Damian just as Mass is beginning. The priest and the Franciscan-robed altar server are at the altar when we exchange the sign of peace with those around us.

The priest and the altar boy receive Communion and conclude the Mass immediately, with no Communion being offered. I approach the altar server and request Communion in my best Italian, holding out my hand and repeating, "Jesu Christi, Holy Communion". He is emphatic in his response that it is for Father only, and I need to come back tomorrow at eight o'clock. Exasperated, I look at him with my new-found Italian arms waving in the air, and shout, "No future in your church — no future at all!" as I storm out.

As I say, it is a defining moment for me.

Early the next morning in the Vatican, I am surprised to see Popes John XXIII and Pius XII lying in state. We have seen Catherine of Siena in another church closer to where we are staying.

I am overwhelmed by the ceilings, domes, artwork and mosaic floors of St Peter's and the Sistine Chapel. On our walk we pass several older women in black clothes, sitting on the footpath begging. Their veils are pulled over their heads as they wail and call out to the tourists. One in particular is not receiving any donations, and starts whacking the footpath furiously with her stick. It's a hot day, made even hotter by the crowds in the Sistine Chapel. Surprisingly, we find a bar in the chapel building and rest under the wisteria with a beer.

Many of the buildings in the centre of Rome are covered in graffiti; this surprises me in this city of ornate architecture; however, on the night bus tour the statues and monuments are lit up and look suitably dramatic. The graffiti is no longer evident.

On Sunday morning we board the train to Leonardo da Vinci airport to meet our friend Pip. When she finally appears we hug and cry and sit down for the first of many croissants and coffees. Being together again in this exotic destination makes it more exciting.

We look ahead an Italian adventure, beginning with Jack driving the upgraded rental car along the ring road towards Firenze. Our stationwagon is missing a side mirror, but the rental car person reassures us saying, "Si, Si, you have full cover if anything else falls off, don't worry!"

Pip and Joanne.

We head north, stopping at Spoleto and Assisi.

God's palette of colours changes so much in each country, and Italy in early summer has my favourite blues and greens. Spoleto is enchanting. The maze of alleyways, potted plants and shutters and the ancient buildings in shades of beige or hokey-pokey nestle against the muted blue-green of the countryside and the silvery greys of the olive leaves. Spoleto has a beautiful church; when we arrive during Mass, this time the people are invited to share communion!

We are strolling down one of the steep lanes when Pip thrusts her arm out towards two men approaching and says, "Buck Shelford — Pip Nicholls, New Zealand!" Buck, a former All Black, is with Murray Deaker, a New Zealand sports radio host. We stop to ask their views on why New Zealand missed out on co-hosting the rugby World Cup. Murray is emphatic that the three reasons were naivety, arrogance and greed. We tell Buck about the 'Bring Back Buck' sign hanging from a Dublin flat when the All Blacks were there. He is amused, and surprised that this humorous campaign is international.

The lush, early summer Italian countryside reminds me of the green-blue Wairarapa hills and fields in the same season, before the sun has burnt them brown. We follow St Claire's footsteps and continue further around the hill to Assisi, where we run into Gerry, a New Zealand priest we know. It is a day for meeting Kiwis in Italy.

I can feel the driver's testosterone rise with each kilometre on the autostrada. The speed and cheek of the Italian drivers means the only option is to keep up with them. The car responds well to the demand, as does driver Jack. As the sun is setting we leave the Siena road at Bargino and wind several kilometres along one dirt road, then another, and a final 500 metres down a hilly dirt track to arrive at Casa Fallochhio, our Tuscan villa. We are staying in the Torre apartment, the tower at the top of the stone farmhouse. I long for my sister Claire and friend Huia, long-time Tuscany aficionados, to share what I see and feel as we drive in.

We spend our whole week in Toscana being very Italian, a lifestyle that suits me well. The pace of life is perfect, with delectable food and wine, and many siestas. The locals work hard in the morning and again in the late afternoon; about 4 p.m. I notice elderly couples strolling in the sun or bending over the vegetable patch. Pip and I virtually move into Mario's *alimentari* in the village of San Pancrazio, an exquisite deli selling fresh breads and cheeses, vegetables and delicious Italian ice cream. Mario and Steffi have a two-month-old baby, Sophia. Every morning we walk two kilometres up the hill, past the olive groves and vineyards, to enjoy our croissant and *caffè latte* sitting on the footpath outside it. From here we watch the villagers arriving to buy bread, ham, cheese or the freshest tomatoes.

Mario is a tall, dark man with a hooked nose; he looks French. His mother comes down to hold the baby and cajole her into sleep. Sometimes Mario sits there with us, murmuring over and over to the baby, *"Si, Si"* and falling asleep himself as he holds her. We sit there, just melting at how incredibly Italian the whole scene is.

San Gimignano homes.

The *alimentari* is at the busy crossroads of the village, so there's always something to watch. Across the road is the small and beautiful church where I discover a large painting of the breastfeeding Madonna, *Madonna del Latte*.

At noon on 25 April (Anzac Day in New Zealand and Australia) the bells from all the churches within a five-kilometre radius ring — amid the olive trees and vineyards and the blue irises and red poppies on show for the Angelus on Liberation Day. And after the siesta we wander back up the hill for a *gelato*. We sit outside Mario's again and take in the activities at the close of day. The rhythm of life in rural Italy is just right.

The Monday market in San Casciano Val di Pesa is eight kilometres away. We arrive in time to buy the best cooking ingredients: fresh vegetables, cheeses, bread, sausages and pasta. We prefer to cook at home, supplemented with our twice-daily visits to Mario's, where the *gelato* is the best.

The Torre apartment is enormous, light and airy. Dark wooden beams hold up the ceiling and the floors are bare, with rugs over terracotta tiles. The bathroom is completely white with a white lace cotton curtain at the window. Eight enormous white bath towels rolled up with sprigs of fresh lavender were waiting for us when we arrived. Our bedroom is nearly double the size of our Dublin apartment, and furnished in sea-greens. The walls are all white except where butterflies have been painted on the wall above the bed. In one corner is a writing desk, and a sea-green cane chair in the other. The windows open out so we can hear the birds singing day and night. The nightingale sings incessantly one night and Jack tapes its song for a friend who shares his love of birds.

A winding spiral staircase with a thick cream cord handrail leads up to the tower,

Madonna del Latte and the altar at the church of San Pancrazio.

which is Pip's bedroom. This room has tall windows overlooking the terracotta roof tiles that are covered in moss and lichen, and beyond to the surrounding fields, olive groves and vineyards. The modest kitchen space downstairs looks up the dusty white road that brought us here. Our lounge is enormous and we can also use the communal kitchen.

The estate is in the Chianti district, about 16 kilometres south of Firenze, 39 kilometres north of Siena and 40 from Pisa. Every day we choose another part of Toscana to explore from this central location. My favourite is San Gimignano, an exquisite medieval walled town with thirteen towers, which my niece Emma has told us not to miss.

Lucca is another walled town, famous for its olive oil. I am in Lucca on the internet when I get an email from my nephew Sam saying baby Kahu (who had been kidnapped) has been found alive and well. I cross the road to St Zita's church and light a candle to thank God for her safe return. I find a card of St Zita for my friend Kathleen, who astounded us all as ten year olds by choosing Zita as her confirmation name.

I am enraptured with rural Italy and dream of returning again and again.

Back in Dublin, Jec has prepared a fine welcome home dinner for the Italian travellers. Pip soon settles into touring Dublin, exploring her O'Connell clan history and spending time with her niece Sarah. Helen and Kevin host a dinner in her honour. A visit to Newgrange and Glendalough is included of course, and

Torre apartment, Casa Fallocchio, and the view from the bedroom.

Pip and Jack walk around the coast from Bray to Greystones. Our apartment reminds Pip of living in New York city, popping downstairs for a newspaper, bagel and coffee.

We are all disappointed when our plans for a six-day tour around Ireland are disrupted by an acute problem with two discs in my back. After seeing the pain I'm in, the doctor calls an ambulance. In the end it's four Dublin firemen in navy blue shirts and trousers, with white gloves, who stretcher me down two flights of stairs into the ambulance. I am home from St Vincent's Hospital within a few hours. The valium injection in my back and other medication mean I am able move gingerly about the apartment for the next week.

Pip and Jack go north to the Holy Hill Monastery in Sligo and stay overnight in the hermitage, meeting Pip's friends from her time in a monastery in Nova Scotia. They tour Donegal together for another three days while Jessica nurses me at home. Though I feel sad at missing this adventure with Pip, two herniating discs make the decision to remain at home straightforward. I am only too thankful it didn't happen in Italy.

Once the heavy cocktail of drugs is finished, homeopathic remedies and gentle physiotherapy over several weeks slowly restore my back. I visit a doctor near Grafton Street who reminds me of my midwife friend Joan, in New Zealand. After organising the referral for physiotherapy, the doctor smiles as I leave and says, "Now mind y'self, Jewarne, and God bless."

It has been great to reconnect with Pip and enjoy Italy and Ireland with her. And saying goodbye to her at the airport is for only a few weeks.

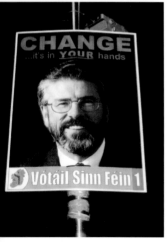

The abortion referendum is confusing. Both sides offer absolute protection to the unborn child, urging voters to vote Yes or No to guarantee this protection. The voting system is archaic and can make it difficult to vote. If for example you live in Kerry but work in Dublin, you must vote in Kerry. The election is on a Friday, and though the booths are open until late and many travel home to vote, some do not bother.

Billboards on Bachelors Walk.

You are only eligible to vote in one specified polling booth, which is identified on a card that comes in the letter box. Jack is only able to vote at Brunswick St. There appear to be no special votes, as we have in New Zealand, for voters away from home.

Work is busy. I have a lot of catching up to do after my holiday in Italy and the time waiting for my back to improve. In my taxi to one of the hospitals for an early meeting, the taxi driver says he is supporting Sinn Féin in the election, and we have an interesting chat. Gerry Adams is an intelligent and astute politician compared to many others appearing on TV each night. The taxi driver questions how the Greens can use plastic tape to put their posters up and maintain their integrity. His car radio is reporting an incident on a bus and the bus drivers' recent strike over concerns about their own safety and that of the passengers. "Do you tink dat incident was de straw dat broke de camel's back?" the interviewer asks the bus driver.

"Well, the ting is. Yer camel has eight or nine humps, and dis would've only broken one of dem if yer see what I mean!"

I will miss my taxi rides when I return to New Zealand, and I also wonder how I can bring home with me the buzz of walking across the city bridges or home to Grafton Street.

Hymn for a tiny grandchild

We knew you as our Easter egg
And called you this with love
We stand beside your parents now
You shine in skies above

Herbert Park is wild and windy
Lashed by a wild spring storm
The pond frozen at New Year
Is covered in petals from blooms

Our seasons changed as well
Our Easter egg has gone
Your star above looks bright
But a long way from home

We thank God for your life
Special, sweet but brief
We say goodbye with tears
Our hearts are full of grief

20 May 2002

Kiwi update, May

Ahakoa iti, he pounamu (Although small, it is precious)

We are having the saddest week, needing to be closer to Hannah and Michael as they come to terms with the loss of the little baby they were carrying — it is a mystery and a gift how much joy a tiny unborn human being can bring to the world in the course of fourteen short weeks. We know they are surrounded by wonderful family and friends, including an exceptional group of aunties. We have always called this wee baby the Easter egg, as we first heard about it as we left for Scotland on Holy Thursday. Our sadness now matches the joy of that day.

21

OLÉ! OLÉ! OLÉ!

Jack has been studying archaeology at the University of Dublin. His course includes a three-day field trip to ancient sites, including Fermanagh where his grandfather was born. While he is away I spend the weekend at Jiff and Lew's apartment on my own, reading, knitting, watching Michael Campbell win the golf and mourning the loss of our grandchild. Their bed feels just right for my back and I appreciate the generous offer of the peace and space of their home once again. The park below is full of cygnets and ducklings, and rhododendrons in full bloom.

When I hear that Mary Robinson has lit a candle on her kitchen windowsill for the millions of souls that make up the Irish diaspora, I feel included and welcomed by this eloquent gesture. Many McPadden and Doherty 'seedlings' have grown in New Zealand from original Irish stock.

My great-grandfather Myles left County Leitrim during the famine and married Bridget Clune from Quin in County Clare.

A candle to welcome us home.

They started a new life on the West Coast of New Zealand, running a hotel near Westport. Here they welcomed other Irish immigrants and made them feel at home in this part of New Zealand where the climate is similar to that of Ireland. Myles and Bridget later milked cows on the banks of the Buller River. My other great-grandmother, Catherine, is buried on the West Coast too and her headstone reads, "A native of Donegal".

It is now a year since we arrived in Ireland. We left home to come home. I will think of Ireland as 'home — lower case', and among the myriad experiences and emotions of my time here I will remember to thank Mary Robinson. When we drive through Phoenix Park at dusk, I see the candle alight on the windowsill of Aras an Uachtarain, the home of the President.

Ireland played gallantly in the 2002 Football World Cup in Japan and Korea. I have been brought up on rugby in a sports-mad country, but there is no comparison with the passion and commitment of the Irish to their national sport. When the All Blacks toured Ireland last October, we tentatively displayed our black flag with the silver fern in the window of our apartment, but the pride and passion evident in the flags and buntings appearing everywhere over the last month makes a confident statement about what it means to be Irish.

Jack's cousin Pip and her husband Pat arrive just as the city is being adorned in orange, white and green banners in support of players at the World Cup. One house on the Liffey has the entire façade painted in the Irish tricolour. Our visitors are in no doubt as to which country they have landed in! The taxis, houses and offices are decorated with bunting or flags.

There is a furore because Roy Keane has been sent home from Japan by the coach, Mick McCarthy. Half the country says the decision is a national disaster and a wreath has been laid at the Football Association rooms. The first game in Japan is at 7.30 a.m. Irish time. It is a Saturday, so Jack hopes to be at Fitzsimon's Bar across the Liffey. It would be far too

The home of an avid football fan.

boring to watch it at home and miss the atmosphere of the Dublin crowds. On the bus coming home from visiting friends in the suburb of Knocklyon, the driver has the radio blaring, with callers giving opposing views on Mick McCarthy's decision. We ask the driver if callers are in favour of the captain or the coach. Who is out of line? The bus driver is more than happy to park the bus and give us his opinion while passengers wait to get off. Last night's headlines read: "MICK EXTEND THE HAND". Tonight's headlines read: "ROY, PICK UP THE PHONE!"

The bus driver assures us that although Roy Keane is the best player, he has crossed the line by abusing and disrespecting the coach and other players. We hear Roy complaining in his Cork accent about the preparations being substandard — no balls to practise with, no high-salt drinks for the heat, and the practice surface like a "cow pat" to run on. However, due to his accent, I think Roy is actually saying carpark, not cow pat. When I first came to Ireland I found the Cork accent difficult but now I recognise it immediately and it is one of my favourites. One council member is from Cork and he often asks me about New Zealand or the All Blacks, and I used to just nod or ask him several times what he was saying, but now if I really listen I can hold quite a conversation.

The football games have been enormous fun. Marion and I watch one in the pub across the road from St James Hospital. It's packed with people of all ages in green T-shirts and green hats, standing on chairs and sitting on the mantelpiece or anywhere they can glimpse the big screen. Many hospital workers have taken an early lunch break. "Is that haematology over there?" one woman asks as she arrives, looking around for her colleagues.

The crowd in the pub sings the national anthem and the whistle blows. When the first Irish player touches the ball and begins to kick it down the field, the woman next to me begins her commentary, laced with many a "fook" and "yer fooker", directed at either the referee or the German opposition. After her initial outburst she grabs my arm and asks, "You're not too squeamish standing next to me, are yer love?" I wish I could tape her match-winning performance, and at the end of the game, a victory for the Irish, she throws her arms around me saying, "See you next Tuesday, love!" We are friends for life.

I am a committed Irish football fan. By the next game I am wearing a green T-shirt with 'Ireland' on the front and the flag is hanging in our apartment window. The partying and craic go on all day and all night in Temple Bar. I learn the words to 'C'mon You Boys in Green', and 'All You Need is Duff' from the revellers on the footpath under my bedroom window, and by the second game I have progressed to sorting out which particular 'Keano' I am chanting for after the sensational first week of the tournament (there are two in the team).

The next two games are just as enthralling. Crammed into an office with a large television set and several work colleagues, I watch Ireland play Cameroon. Marian's teddies, our mascots, are on top of the television. We scream and yell as goals are scored and the final whistle sees Ireland's hopes still very much alive. The atmosphere in the city is electric that evening, especially at Gogarty's in Temple Bar. A livewire band plays and the crowd sings and dances for hours. When the band stops for a break, the crowd raises the flag above their heads. At 5 a.m. they are still singing under our windows. I am not sure what the absentee rate in Ireland must be the next day, as even Jack and I confess to feeling very sleepy at our desks.

The babies and young children in town are all in the Irish colours. I see babies with green and orange hats, green blankets and clothes and booties and Irish flags tied to their prams. It reminds to me that we need to change our flag in New Zealand quickly to one that is more relevant and meaningful to us.

Pip and Pat have an rich time here in Ireland discovering their families and ancestors and visiting the places they came from. Though my back keeps me in Dublin, I am pleased to hear how they discover that Pat's mum's family and Pip's mum's family are buried in the same cemetery in Northern Ireland, west of Derry. I hear on his return how Jack met Pip and Pat in Enniskillen and they stayed at Frank and Eileen's, then travelled to Derry and Donegal together. A chatty Irishman in a Derry pub thought Jack was Crocodile Dundee and Pip was Kylie Minogue; "small but perfectly formed" were his words. Pat recalled that his glasses were like the bottoms of milk bottles, and he had been at the bar several hours. When Pat

Owners and trainers at the Dublin Horse Fair.

had asked if anyone swam round these parts, the man had nodded saying, "only the members of the Polar Bear Club."

My back has recovered enough to join the others for fish and chips at Howth after exploring the Boyne Valley, and to visit the horse fair in Dublin. This is held one Sunday a month and horses of all shapes and sizes stand untethered beside their equally quirky owners. It is a real Dublin experience; one man is eager for us to buy his donkey to take back to New Zealand.

We will miss Pip and Pat; they have revelled in their "first of many" visit to Ireland. Pat has cooked dinner for us every night after work, even though we refer to him as "your royal highness". This is not just because he's so tall, but because of his royal O'Neill heritage, which even Jack concedes is more prestigious than the Doherty clan. Pip and Pat will be in Spain when Ireland plays Spain on Sunday. They will enjoy the celebrations, although it is highly unlikely that Ireland will win that game.

They are interviewing people on the radio today about the football. One man says they finally managed to get to Korea but it involved taking a small plane, a train, a ride on a slow boat, then another train. Joe Duffy asked the man how much all this was costing him. "Well Joe, the cost is immaterial — you see, we're here for the World Cup, not the cost!" It may be a good thing that divorce is now legal here, because the men are phoning home for loans and the credit unions and

Should we take this one home to New Zealand?

Lew and Jack, the Southside versus the Northside.

banks have been besieged with toll calls from Japan so the Irish supporters can travel to Korea for the next game. None of them wants to come home. Ireland was not expected to proceed to the next round, in the same way France and Argentina were not expected to be returning home so early.

One caller rings Joe to say it is cheaper for him to fly back to Ireland and set out again to fly to Korea than pay the price he has been quoted to fly from Japan to Korea. I'm not sure how the Japanese Guinness flows, but the craic on the radio from Irish supporters in Japan is most entertaining.

More friends, Kath and John, arrive soon after Pip and Pat leave. They flew into Derry from London and found a pub in Lifford just across the Donegal border to watch the football. It turns out to be the local pub of Shay Given, the goalkeeper. The ardent local supporters chant *"O Shay, O Shay, O Shay!"* instead of *"Olé, Olé, Olé!"* They arrive in Dublin from Donegal late one Friday evening after visiting friends of their son's in Oldcastle in County Meath.

When Ireland walk out to play Spain the cobblestone lanes of Temple Bar are empty. It is hot and humid, with a record crowd both in Fitzsimon's Bar and in the stadium in Korea.

We watch the game dressed in green with several hundred other fans, who sing and drink as the tension mounts. Extra time comes and goes. It feels like the longest two hours of my life, and then the final outcome — Ireland is out of the Cup.

The crowd, after a few seconds of silence and disbelief, clap and roar loudly and sing another few choruses of 'C'mon You Boys in Green'. Two hours later we spill out of the pub and watch as the crowds continue to dance and party even though Ireland has lost.

We go to a concert at the Olympia Theatre to raise funds for the special Olympics being held in Ireland. Sinead O'Connor sings an unaccompanied version of 'Molly Malone', and the theatre is hushed. As we walk home through Temple Bar we discover about 200 people dancing on the cobblestones to the singing of Hugh, a Maori from the Waikato. Kath requests 'Ten Guitars', which means we four Kiwis are the only ones dancing, singing and aged over forty! When Hugh

stops for a break the young Irish dance and wave their flags above their heads, chanting and singing 'You'll Never Beat The Irish'. Reading the media the next day it is difficult to detect that Ireland is out of the World Cup. The headlines read:

"They left as heroes — they came home as gods."

"Damien Duff did all but levitate."

Damien's mum is interviewed about Padre Pio, whose impending canonisation could not top the soccer headlines. He has been important to Damien. His mum is dressed in a kimono, and is sad she can't be in Korea to give her boy a hug.

We reflect that when the All Blacks played poorly in the first rugby test against Ireland, the score did not reflect the game, and Kiwis booed their own heroes off the field. The Italian soccer fans in Melbourne rioted in the streets when their team was out of the World Cup. Later the Italian club sacked the Korean player who had scored the golden goal against Italy. But the Irish can teach the world how to celebrate effort and commitment in sport even when you lose.

I do breathe a sigh of relief on Monday morning; life in Dublin, and my sleep patterns, may return to normal. However it is announced there will be a Welcome Home for the Boys in Green in Phoenix Park the next evening. We head along the quays on the buses, flags flying out the windows and passengers of all ages singing football songs together. On our way to the park we pass a man walking with his donkey draped in the Irish flag.

We stroll through the long summer grass towards the big screen as long lines of people spread out across the park. They come from every direction, marching across the fields. We sit in the long grass beside many families, one with a boxer dog in a tight-fitting T-shirt with 'Ireland' across the back.

The end of my first World Cup football experience, singing 'The Fields of Athenry' with 100,000 others, makes me tingle with emotion and never want to leave this land. Go Ireland!

The BBC has an hour every night this week from the Chelsea Flower Show. One gold medal winner is an Irish woman from Wicklow who designed a Celtic sanctuary garden around a pond with huge stone thrones. A fire burns in the middle of the water and a ring of stones form the outer edge. When Prince Charles stops to look at the garden he is invited to try out one of the thrones. This magical garden is now relocated to the new hospice in Blackrock, County Dublin, where it gives endless pleasure to the patients, their families and the staff.

We are trying to think of everything we want to do in our remaining three months here. My position has been advertised, to Helen's dismay, but she is also supportive and understanding of my need to return home. I am pleased I can finish my twelve-month contract and present two major reports to the June and July Council meeting, which will include recommendations and plans of action for implementation. The Council has introduced a successful strategy and accessed resources to reduce the Ear Nose & Throat waiting times for children. I can see that much has been achieved by the three paediatric hospitals this past year. I have enjoyed working alongside so many committed health professionals, and Helen's chairing of the Council has ensured the focus has remained on improving the health of children and their access to the services they need.

Jack attends a health conference on empowerment with 250 nurses. He is asked to be the raconteur who captures the dialogue and discussion at the end of the day. He is introduced with a brief biography, ending with, "But we all know that with a name like Doherty, he is of course, a Donegal boy too!" For Jack this is the ultimate recognition.

John and Kath are in Kerry meeting their O'Sullivan relations and will return to Dublin on Friday, the same day my oldest best friend, Patsy, arrives.

Anthem

Our love was on the wing
We had dreams and songs to sing

Being here with you
In Ireland — homeland
Is one of the dreams

We are singing the songs
There are more to come
For us to sing and dream
Thank you

KIWI UPDATE, JUNE

We hear that an election has been called in New Zealand and understand we may be able to vote electronically from Dublin.

I can't believe Alice is having yet another teacher strike day. What's the craic there? Reading the news online, I detect that parental and student opinion may be turning against the teachers' stand. The New Zealand weather sounds extreme: Jude's car needed to be towed by a tractor in the South Island snow, and Matthew rang John and Kath to say the snow has cut the electricity supply and he is not sure how he will milk 300 cows.

Josh and Roze have celebrated their birthdays and started antenatal classes in preparation for their baby's birth.

Jules sends us an excellent report of the Te Wakaiti annual meeting and I receive a special card from baby Kahu's whanau.

Gid and Paul send a letter and the booklet from Olive's funeral including a wonderful photo of three of my sisters, Gid, Pip and Ma, all with shovels at the burial taking their turn, with Kate, John and Chris looking on — a photo worth a thousand words. The whole week has been a great farewell to a special lady but we will miss her, especially on Christmas Day and at the Tauherenikau races.

Hannah and Alice are hanging out for the school holidays. It sounds as if we won't recognise Hannah and Michael's home on our return with all the changes. Alice is counting the days and weeks until we arrive home. Her friend Ben's mum is coming to stay two nights in Dublin with us. Robyn has been lovely to Alice this year, so it will be nice to repay her hospitality.

Quin Abbey, County Clare.

22

Patsy O'Reilly Explores Ireland

Patsy and I have been best friends since we were ten, so her visit is a gift. For 40 years I have found myself waiting for Patsy and missing buses or the first half of films. I remember the sailors replacing the gangplank for her on a tramping trip thirty years ago, after she missed the ferry to the South Island by one minute. I will head to Dublin airport and wait with open arms and see what happens. Patsy, Pip and I all turn 50 this year, so we are creating a fund of memories of our Irish and Italian adventures together.

Patsy looks remarkably fresh and un-jetlagged. This is possibly because she missed her first flight when she left home with an expired passport, and arrived in Dublin 24 hours late. When Lucy, her daughter, rings to tell me her mum will be a day late I laugh out loud, thinking she is teasing me. But after 40 years of waiting for Patsy, another day won't matter.

She arrives the same evening John, Kath and Sarah fly back to London. Our Shoebox is chaotic as suitcases are packed and unpacked, sheets washed and dried and beds remade. It's a fun couple of hours as the visitors overlap.

Patsy acquaints herself with Dublin while I go to work. Central Dublin is compact and easy to find your way about. She enjoys the bus tour of the city, hopping on and off to explore any nooks and crannies that take her eye, and finds that striking up conversations with Dubliners is always a great investment in a bit of craic.

A Dublin highlight for the three of us is The Dubliners' 40th anniversary concert. We are three rows from the stage and underneath lights and cameras, as this concert is being filmed. When I order the video several months later back home in New Zealand, there are several scenes of us singing along and swaying in our seats to the music.

I am able to take annual leave during Patsy's visit, so we collect a rental car and set out, beginning with day trips from Dublin. Jack is with us for the first three days in the Boyne Valley touring Newgrange, the Slane Abbey ruins and Cavan, the home of the O'Reilly ancestors. At the O'Reilly Castle ruin, several teenagers spending the afternoon together include two O'Reillys, amused to meet this 'cousin' from New Zealand.

We ask how old his cottage is. "Four," he says, then after a pause, "four centuries."

On our way through Westmeath we stop outside an exquisite thatched cottage and chat to the man who lives there. We ask how old his cottage is. "Four," he says, then after a pause, "four centuries." We drive via Oldcastle to Fore, where there are fifth-century abbey ruins that once were home to over 3000 monks.

I leave Patsy and Jack exploring the abbey and go up the road to buy one of Mrs O'Reilly's homemade chocolate cakes. When they return to the car, thermos tea and surprise cake are waiting on the picnic table.

The castle in the film *Braveheart* is in Trim, and near the castle we find a little old lady in a floral raincoat crossing the road from her cottage to throw her fishing line into the river. After a few minutes with her discussing fishing, we end our day with fish and chips on the pier at Howth.

Next day, south of Dublin, we stop for a wet picnic under the umbrellas near Dalkey before heading to Glendalough.

The sun comes out between the showers as we stroll up to the lakes and St Kevin's cell, and Patsy and I both have a sleep on the damp grass after talking late last night.

On our way to Derry next day we stop to watch the World Cup football final before showing Patsy the Grianán of Aileach. We share benediction with the parish in the church — designed to complement the ring fort — that won an architectural award for the building of the century.

Patsy at Newgrange.

We visit Doherty Keep in Buncrana after walking the city walls of Derry and visiting Letterkenny. Patsy is highly amused at the look of the school in Letterkenny that Alice never quite enrolled at; in fact, she takes a photo of anything she sees that is desprit. Patsy is an educationist, and is surprised to see the dreary grey school buildings that look like a penal institution. They often have no decoration, style or colour and few windows — presumably to conserve the heat.

We drive on through Donegal and stay in Glenties, spending the evening in a pub, entertained by a Northern Irish woman who sings and plays the harp. It is Patsy's turn to meet Hugh and Philomena in their shop in Ardara, a must-see for all our visitors after Newgrange, Glendalough, Derry and the Grianán of Aileach. We are there for the best part of two hours and the craic is ninety. Hugh swears vigorously and pops out the back continuously to check his horse-racing outcomes.

His mammy Philomena is reluctant to part with anything in the shop. "Ah no, that is mine!" she wails if she hears me asking the price of anything. Hugh tells us some tourists can't relate to the fact that the shop is full of treasures she won't part with, and they storm out the door. But I totally understand how she feels.

Patsy wants to buy a green frog for her daughter Sophie. He lies on his side, leaning on an elbow, and is dressed in a striped jersey. Philomena is devastated. "He's been my friend for years," she wails.

"Ah Mammy, we're not running a fookin' orphanage — there's plenty more upstairs," says Hugh with a wink.

Patsy wants to know if the frog croaks, so Hugh pokes it and throws it on the wooden floor saying, "I'll fookin' show you croak!" As he wraps our purchases he throws in

Glendalough, County Wicklow.

Donegal socks and minuscule leprechauns and shamrocks. Then he announces he has no idea what to charge, "so just make it sixty euros."

On an islet in Lough Derg Jack is spending the traditional three-day retreat or 'cultural' experience known as 'Patrick's Purgatory'. I am far too rebellious to go there myself. Patsy and I stay on the mainland at the edge of the lake, watching the little boat take Jack to the island.

A tiny Irishman appears and asked how long we will be parked as this is not the proper carpark. His nametag introduces him as 'Patsy' (a common name for a man in Ireland), so I ask him to meet my friend of the same name. This is the start of a riotous trip for Patsy and me as we head south to Sligo, looking for the Holy Hill Hermitage our friend Pip is keen for us to visit.

Holy Hill is a Carmelite community for men and women; it has only been in Ireland since the late 1990s, and has stone hermitages which used for retreats. A man called Eric shows us the projects the community has completed since they arrived and began work at the ruins of the convent. My favourite places are the new internal garden, and a gravel pit for an outside fire. They consiously make use of the elements of creation, work and play as part of their mode of prayer. The community has commissioned a statue of the Madonna that expresses her humanity. In the garden is a delightful sculpture of Mary playing with a four or five-year-old Jesus, who is chasing a dog that leaps in the air. We see the hermitage where Pip and Jack stayed, and leave Holy Hill a few hours later, feeling we know Pip better after visiting one of her spiritual sources.

As we drive out through the gate, I declare to Patsy, "I am heading for a quieter decade."

The grey stone mill in Westport, County Mayo is now the old Mill Hostel. Bright red windows punctuate its sheer walls. We arrive after a long day of driving. We two tired women squeeze our car under the stone archway and follow the shy young Irishman up several flights of stairs. He shows us the dormitory, and seven German faces look up as we walk in.

After soup and Irish bread, we spend the evening in the back bar of Matt Malloy's pub. Matt Malloy is the flute player in the Chieftains and Michael, an

The Old Mill Hostel, Westport, County Mayo.

older man, is singing unaccompanied some of his 300 ballads. His pub is made up of several intimate bars, but the bar with Michael singing his ballads is the best one tonight.

Westport is bright and alive, with decorative shopfronts. Many of the towns, like the Dublin suburbs, have been decorated in the last month with window boxes and hanging baskets overflowing with petunias, lobelias and pansies. Pasty bought Jack petunias for the window box on Bachelors Walk, "just to brighten up your last seven weeks in Ireland," she said. The flower colours here are more vivid in the absence of our strong New Zealand sunlight. I have been stopping at the flower stalls to smell the scent of stock that reminds me of my mum Tui, and I have decided to grow stock on my return to New Zealand, along with the sweet peas that I hope will grow like those I saw in Scotland.

Next morning we journey through Muckross near Croagh Patrick. We make a half-hearted attempt to climb the mountain and meet three Irish women saying the rosary at the base of the climb, holding on to walking sticks and each other as they begin their ascent. Across the road is a graphic sculpture of a Coffin Ship,

and above this boat and under the sails are strips tied together. Only when I go closer do I see these are skeletons holding onto each other.

The drive towards Connemara is around the lakes and the grey and white Connemara stone pokes through the earth wherever it can. Kylemore Abbey in the early evening is still and a perfect reflection lies on the lake. We join the Benedictine nuns for vespers at 6 p.m. I daren't sit by Patsy, or catch her eye, as the nuns' high voices begin to sing the psalms.

The coffin ship at Muckross, County Mayo: "skeletons holding onto each other."

We stand beside St Benedict, holding hands for a photo to send to a young Benedict we know back in New Zealand. Later I buy the Kylemore Abbey cookbook, full of the abbey's favourite recipes with photos of the nuns milking the cows, gardening and farming. Of these three contrasting experiences: benediction in the parish of Burt, prayer at Holy Hill and vespers at Kylemore Abbey, it is Holy Hill I am drawn to return to.

We sleep that night in a hostel at Clifden, upsetting a muttering German woman who does not appreciate our feeble attempts to climb into the top bunks. A young Australian man lends us his torch, saying, "It just might help keep her quiet, mate," as Patsy pushes me and my sore back up the ladder to the top tier. We are hysterical. The hostel bunks are firm and comfortable, but the next morning the German woman starts 'giving out' again as we try to negotiate our descent. Each morning after breakfast we fill our thermos with tea in the hostel kitchens and pack a picnic lunch. Usually we end the day with soup and Irish bread at a pub. It is an inexpensive but perfectly adequate way to travel around Ireland.

We spend the next morning ambling around Clifden. Patsy likes to write her postcards with the scene in front of her, so we stop and enjoy the village before spending another day in the car.

On the grey rock of the Burren, we see one cow and two sheep. Patsy decides it must be lightly stocked for summer. The days are light until after 10.30 p.m. so there is plenty of daylight for travelling and we finally arrive in Doolin, overlooking Galway Bay, late in the evening.

Kylemore Abbey,
County Galway.

Doolin, County Clare.

The hostel is cosy, and comes complete with the Sacred Heart and a 1916 uprising poster. We sleep on a double futon. When we asked yer man how comfy it will be for someone with a sore back, he jumps on it boots and all and says, "Ooh now, it feels grand to me!" It isn't.

In O'Connor's pub, an American woman's T-shirt announces she has walked the Milford Track in New Zealand. She retired at 50 after working in advertising and insurance, and now spends her days singing in the Delphi choir and hiking. German tourists at the pub have walked the Milford Track too and become animated when they realise two real New Zealanders are in their midst. Patsy convinces them we have walked the track many times.

Another wet, cold visit to the Cliffs of Moher, a wave at the Consedine's pub and a visit to St Brigid's Well fill the next morning. At the well, Patsy trips over her camera strap and falls onto a mound of gravel. There are many desprit events like that on our tour, where we laugh and laugh. Patsy's visit is the best tonic for me after being so sad for Hannah, and nursing a painful back for several weeks.

I want to find Quin, near Ennis, from where my great-grandmother Bridget Clune left Ireland to come to New Zealand. The old man at the Quin Post Office says he is a dear friend of Joe Clune. He goes on to say, "Ooh yer man Joe would be a great age now, well past a hundred. Himself would have all the information, y'know."

"Is he still alive then?" I ask, excited about meeting Joe and finding out about my Clune family.

"Ah no, God rest his soul, he's not at all, no." He advises me to look in the Quin Abbey cemetery and tells me where the Clune family homestead is still standing. I spend half an hour under my umbrella at Quin Abbey writing down names of

Clunes, many with the Christian name of Bridget, and one next to the grave of a Josephine Consedine. Later we find the stone cottage, all restored but sinking into the footpath. Nobody is home. The hostels at Killarney are full, so we head to Dingle. This village has a post office, two shops, a pottery shop … and seven pubs! We stay at the Red Fuschia Lodge with our very own bunkroom, surrounded by hedges full of wild red fuschias.

In Dan Foley's pub, balladeer 'Billy the Kid' McKenna is singing by the fire. He offers to serenade us and sings 'Come Back Paddy Reilly to Ballyjamesduff' for Patsy when her hears she's an O'Reilly from Cavan, and a Donegal song for me, followed by 'The Town I Loved So Well', the song of Derry. It is easy to decide to stay a second night in Annascoul.

At the pub we meet a woman called Margaret, who has three adult sons and

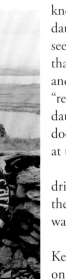

Valencia Island.

knows everyone and everything. "Did you hear the doctor's daughter's marriage was off now?" she asks us. We have seen a wedding in Dingle that day but she assures us that that one was the publican's daughter's wedding. Later, she and her friend go into fits of laughter when I ask about the "republican's daughter's wedding" instead of the publican's daughter. When we leave the pub a dog is lying in the doorway and Margaret comes rushing out with us, yelling at the dog, "Feck off, feck off, feck! feck! feck!"

The sun comes out as we wander around Dingle, then drive around Slea Head and the peninsula, overlooking the Blasket Islands and the fields where *Ryan's Daughter* was filmed.

It is raining next day as we head towards the Ring of Kerry and out to Valencia Island. There is a charity bike race on to raise money for people with intellectual disabilities, and the narrow road that normally struggles with a car or two, let alone the tourist buses, is full of cyclists. Passing five cyclists spreading themselves across the road is stressful, so it is a relief to detour to the island of Valencia where our son Jude lived and worked a couple of years ago. It is a beautiful island, and we spend a few minutes in the Lighthouse Café admiring the mosaic floor he helped create. We eat our lunch at the seashore where the ferry leaves for Caherciveen, which is where my friend Kath's O'Sullivan cousins live. When I place our New Zealand families and friends on the map of Ireland, I see we just about have the place covered. It is no wonder I feel so at home here.

Patsy and I stop for an ice cream in Bandon and check the directions to Cork, as we have deviated from the main route. An old man in the street thinks long and hard before saying, "Ooh now, I can't help ye. I have no idea where Cork is or how to get there from here." We learn from someone else that Cork is only 43 miles from Bandon, so we find the correct road and have a quick tour through Cork and Cobh in the heavy rain before stopping for the night in Youghal (pronounced 'Yo-wall') a quaint seaside resort town. The hostel is newly renovated and the eight-month-old baby of the young mother running the hostel has been sick all day. She looks relieved to hear her two guests have ten children between them and are happy to give advice if needed.

We are heading home to Dublin, listening intently to the radio account of Kiwi Michael Campbell's win in the European Golf Open in Kildare as we drive past the golf course at Dunmore East (a seaside cove of thatched cottages close to Corbally in County Waterford, where Jack's mother's family of Phelans and Kirwans are from). We also hear that the New Zealand Ireland Association is holding a hangi for the New Zealand women's cricket team. This is an unexpected way to end our tour of Ireland, the Kiwis winning all three cricket games including one Jack has watched in the grounds of Trinity College.

We spend Patsy's last day in Dublin with our friend Robyn at the Mercy House in Baggot Street, the original home of the founder, Catherine McCauley, who is buried there in a crypt. We had all been taught by the Sisters of Mercy in New Zealand. In the evening we see *Ragus*, a show performed by a song and dance group from the Aran Islands.

There have been Kiwis visiting for the last seven weeks and the Shoebox has been full. I farewell Patsy and tell her to go on ahead and put the kettle on for a

Dingle peninsula, County Kerry.

cup of tea, as I will be home soon. Jack and I leave Ireland in less than fifty days. I feel wildly excited, but am surprised by the growing lump in my throat when I think of saying goodbye to this land and its people.

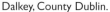

Kiwi update, August

Josh and Roze, Alice, Jude, Hannah and Michael are excited about our homecoming, and are already planning the first day's reunion.

My sister Maree is returning to Nelson after her year in Wellington. We smile when we think about why I wasn't there when she finally did come back to Wellington for a year.

Dalkey, County Dublin.

Silent Valley, County Down.

23

SLÁINTE! GO RAIMH MAITH AGAT (CHEERS! THANK YOU)

We are always the oldest patrons at the Down Under Bar, and sit among the Kiwis and Australians in a seat in the corner. We manage to secure this spot each time an important game is on because Jack goes early. Tonight the pub seems full of noisy South Africans who soon become more subdued as their team meet the All Blacks. We enjoy the Wellington crowd's reaction to captain Tana Umaga's arrival on the field. I notice white plastic bags blowing around in Wellington's famous wind. We can't quite see Josh and Michael, who are in Jack's front row seats on the half-way line.

Living without a car, we have enjoyed being picked up by friends and taken for exciting drives a few times this year. This Sunday Jiff and Lew take us to Skerries, north of Dublin, with its working windmill, then northwest to Westmeath and a long drive down country lanes to Fore, to see the abbey in the bog of St Fechin that Jack first visited on his archaeology trip.

Strolling around the ancient abbey site we meet the O'Reilly children again. They had found their dog Glenda abandoned at Glendalough when they were on holiday there and they ask Jack, in their Irish accents, to film Glenda performing tricks for the camera. Jane, their mum, says as long as she keeps them well fed, they are happy exploring the ruins of St Fechin.

Abbey at Fore, County Westmeath.

Jane gives me the programme for the Oldcastle Show the next week. The competitions include:

- Three Best Sticks of Rhubarb
- Best Dressed Granny — lady or gent
- Five Brown Eggs
- Best Dog — any breed, handled by a lady
- Best Apron

We have a lot of fun deciding which ones we are most likely to win and it seems both Lew and I may enter the Best Dressed Granny competition.

On Sunday, Bridget, Jack's friend from work, drives us north again across the border to the Navan Fort in Armagh. This ancient earthwork is 240 metres in diameter and was built in 95 BC. We walk slowly around the perimeter and sit for a long time in different places on the hill, connecting with the spiritual reality of the site and in awe at the ancients' mastery of architectural skills. We share a picnic lunch, with tea from the thermos that has been everywhere with us, before heading north again via Newry to Downpatrick. Downpatrick is in County Down, and the new interactive tourist centre tells the fables, legends and true stories about St Patrick. We later wander up the hill to the Cathedral, where it is said St Patrick is buried with St Brigid and St Colmcille. From a rock slab on top of the grave you can see the mountains of Mourne, deep blue and in sharp profile on this sunny day.

I tease Jack as to whether St Colmcille will give his blessing for him to return to New Zealand. He has followed this saint's life and story for a long time because of Colmcille's links to Donegal and the Doherty clan. At this point a couple and two children arrive. The man is Maori, from Christchurch. "Kia ora!" Jack greets him. He beams, and the children run to the car saying, "Mammy, those people are from New Zealand." He lives in County Down with his Irish wife. He and Jack have quite a korero about Jack's time in Ireland. Jack returns to the car, acknowledging this sign of Colmcille's blessing for his return home, and telling me to be very aware of what I ask for!

Dramatic stone walls follow the steep hills through the mountains of the Silent Valley and down to the coast where the mountains of Mourne sweep down to the sea. The huge boulders rest silently on each other. They would never stay upright in New Zealand's wind and weather, or survive our earthquake tremors.

Kilkeel is a loyalist town, decorated with red, white and blue paint on fences, bridges, footpaths and gutters. All the bunting is of the same colours and the plaques of kings and English flags with skull and crossbones proclaim the identity of these people. To me, it isn't Irish. I sense a united Ireland is definitely off the agenda for most of this community.

We share a Kiwi barbecue in the garden of Jackie and Niall and their children, Enya and Tama. Jack, a friend from Wellington, has joined us after the McGlinchey Summer School in Donegal. Jackie is Maori, from Wanganui, and Niall is a Galway storyteller, a junior shanachie, he tells us. The grandparents are arriving the next day from New Zealand. Their children speak Maori, Gaelic and English. Niall has researched New Zealand stories and knows about the Irish rebellion at Addison's Flat near Westport where my great-grandfather Myles McPadden from Leitrim was a publican. After a failed assassination attempt on the Duke of Edinburgh in 1868 the Irish in Westport (New Zealand) held a mock funeral, creating a furore, and this story is recorded in the New Zealand history archives.

We spend our last weekend in Irvinestown, Fermanagh with Eileen and Frank. We call in to see the McPaddens in Manorhamilton and it is sad to hear from Rose that Myles died suddenly a few weeks earlier. Myles was a gardener extraordinaire, and had a spectacular display of roses he had planted in honour of Rose, whom he married when she was sixteen. We are welcomed and treated, as usual, like royalty. We meet a few more grandchildren, including Katie from New York, who later takes us to Myles' grave which is covered in pansies planted in peat. Katie also takes us to meet two of her aunties, Patricia and Eileen. Rose gives us poetry about Myles

and treasured photos and, for Jack, a special gift to bring back to New Zealand — a bottle of the rare 'auld mountain dew'. Rose explains that Myles rubbed the special brew on his legs when they were aching — but not this particular bottle, she stresses! She says Myles would have loved to see us again and how much he would love Jack to take this special brew home to New Zealand. We have our photos taken in the garden of roses.

The Manorhamilton Show is the next day. Rose has donated the Myles McPadden Memorial Cup for the best rose and all the grandchildren are running around the garden picking grandpa's roses, hoping to win the cup! Rose reminds me of my own mum, Tui. She sits holding court with the visitors while her ten children and numerous grandchildren come in and out of the house all day. She is a talented poet and artist, and has recently exhibited 58 of her paintings. Eileen and Frank have provided a welcoming home for us and this final weekend is shared with cousins Teresa and Eddie from Coventry, who are over for a holiday. Jack, Eileen and Teresa explore the Cassidy Rath near Irvinestown, a first visit for the Cassidy cousins. It is the anniversary Mass for their parents, so the families meet for dinner on Saturday and a barbecue on Sunday after Mass.

Jack gets up at dawn to drive to Westport via Sligo to climb Croagh Patrick with the pilgrims. This annual pilgrimage is held on the last Sunday of July. During the barbecue lunch, he sends a text message: "1000s here. Knocked the bastard off. All drenched!" I explain to the Irish cousins about Sir Edmund Hillary's ascent of Mt Everest and the words, now part of New Zealand history, he used to sum up his remarkable climb.

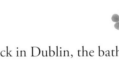

Teresa and Eileen, County Fermanagh.

Back in Dublin, the bathroom door is blocked by four wet umbrellas. In this land, renowned for its rain, we have just been officially told this is the wettest summer on record. This is a cumulative report having been told over the last few months that it has been the wettest April, then May, then June and now July. I am presuming August will follow the same pattern.

We spend a week on holiday in West Cork, staying overnight at Helvick Head in Wexford, then going on to Cobh near Cork to visit the Heritage Centre and its displays depicting the emigrants leaving on the ships. I cry, thinking of

Drombeg stone circle, County Cork.

the way most of our ancestors reached their new homes in America, Australia and New Zealand. Was the sense of adventure of the young ones a match for the grief of their mammies? No email, text messaging or return trips for them.

We arrive in Schull to stay with Helen and Kevin Burke for four nights. Schull is an idyllic harbour of resting yachts that looks out to the Fastnet Rock, famous in yacht racing. We have cherished the friendship and rich company of Helen and Kevin, and finally accept their repeated invitation to holiday with them in West Cork. Kevin prepares delicious three-course gourmet dinners and the first night we dine on soup, wild salmon and rhubarb fool.

Kevin was chief executive of the Irish Seed Potato Industry that exports internationally. One night we offer to cook dinner, but I feel I have lost confidence completely in the peeling, cooking and serving of potatoes in the presence of such an expert. He can name the variety just by looking at the potato, dirt and all!

Their cottage looks out across the garden towards the harbour. We sleep in the 'stables', a single-bedroom chalet that used to house the horses. Helen and Kevin spend about eight weeks here in the summer months and make several shorter visits throughout the year.

One day we go on our own to explore the West Cork coastline, bays dotted with yachts, private castles and villages like Schull, Skibereen and Ballydehob with its twelve-arch bridge. Not far from Skibereen is Clonakilty, where Michael Collins was born. In Skibereen just along from Wee Hannah's Pub we see a hardware shop with a sign painted on the wall: *No coloured paint will be sold to men from this shop unless they produce a note from their wife.* Speaking of colour though, the whole of the countryside in West Cork is a mass of bright red wild fuchsias.

We walk silently around the Drombeg stone circle, known locally as the Druid's Altar. This circle of ancient stones is on a low ridge and, across the green fields, in the distance is the sea.

Mizen Head is the southernmost point of Ireland and the next day we visit with Helen and Kevin. We walk up and down to the lighthouse to see the dolphins and seals, while they read the papers in the sun, and on the way home to Schull we stop for a beer in Crookhaven.

On Sunday we celebrate Mass with Helen and Kevin in Ballydehob. The church has large stained-glass windows and the dark blue wall behind the altar is covered in painted goldfish, all — except one — swimming towards the tabernacle. The altar is an enormous grey rock. It is restful to be in this holy space of old and new.

At Schull I discuss writing with Helen, in particular her collaboration with Olivia O'Leary on Mary Robinson's biography. Helen is a Binchy, and a cousin of Maeve's. They are close friends and Maeve and her husband Gordon are arriving the day we leave, along with Helen's brother and his family — all part of the 'Binchy Invasion' as Helen calls it. I want to leave Maeve a note under the pillow asking her advice about my manuscript, but decide I can't possibly be so 'bold'.

Before we return to Dublin I give Helen a special gift from Aotearoa New Zealand as an expression of my gratitude. This korowai aroha, or cloak of love, is a shawl that appears to be made of feathers but is the softest, brown, speckled fabric

Ballydehob Church, West Cork.

with real feathers sewn in at both ends. Another friend, Christine, has found me the words of poet James K Baxter, writing about unconditional love of a mother hen for her chicks: though there may be lice in her wings, the chicks will come for shelter because there they feel safe.

Helen has provided that space for me during my time in Ireland and honoured me by allowing me to shelter her at times as well. I love her dearly and will miss her when I return to the other side of the world. The gift is perfect for her.

We drive out to Sheep's Head to visit Finn, who ate in our kitchen in New Zealand seven years ago as a dairy farmer visiting on a scholarship. He is surprised to see us again and downs tools for most of the day to show us around Sheep's Head and his family land. Finn is steeped in wisdom beyond his years. His tour includes the ring forts on his family's farm and a souterrain he has recently uncovered with the bulldozer. He is an activist when it comes to the peninsula's heritage and the need to preserve and respect the ancient sites — a view not every newcomer or farmer understands.

He recently helped organise a Christy Moore concert for the locals, as Christy has a house near Kilcrohane. The tickets were only to be sold to locals and Christy requested that the seating be café style and all at the same level so they could enjoy an informal session together. I asked Finn to remember to invite Christy on our behalf, to come to New Zealand again. Towards the end of the day, we headed to Kenmare and over spectacular Molls Gap towards Killarney.

Being Irish

for Jack

I have tasted on your back at night
Atlantic Ocean salt
And smelt again the sweet, sweet smell
Of an Irish peat fire
Trapped in the curls on your head

This land, Ireland,
Has become more of you
Than I first thought
Physical now
To bind the emotional and spiritual

You understand what clan means
Ancient stones and wells
Colmcille greets you
In Ireland
Homeland

The talkback radio is as entertaining as ever. Topics include:
- Women with long hair versus women with short hair
- A decree from the church banning popular songs that aren't traditional hymns
- Pregnancies for women over forty
- First-class relics versus second-class relics

Dolmen in Schull,
County Cork.

- The weather: "Hello Gerry, I'm just back in the country — nice to be here for the monsoon season."
- Travelling people being banned from pubs
- Prayer. One old woman saying, "Well Gerry, I say my morning prayers and that is enough for Him for the day, what with everyting else I need to fit in!"

The weather is always a topic of craic and interaction with the locals. A man at a B&B tells us even the ducks are "giving out about it", and he set three mousetraps last week and caught four trout!

The humour is everywhere. Patsy and I meet a slightly harrassed mother at a café in Dublin. It is the beginning of the wet summer holidays for her four schoolchildren, and she rolls her eyes at the grey sky, saying: "Jesus, would you look at the weather. Yer mun arrived back home with a barbecue for the summer — another ornament, I told him!"

On our way back from Schull to Dublin we stay in the middle of County Cork in Ballyvourney and visit the place where Michael Collins was assassinated. It is soon after the anniversary of his death, and there are a number of messages and poems there, many still referring to him as "the big fella". We drive home to Dublin via Mallow and Limerick.

Returning to Dublin, I immediately miss the fuschias and wild flowers of the country. A week in West Cork has been a superb way to close our time in Ireland, and now it's time to write final reports at work, arrange handover tasks to the new staff and think of packing our bags.

A final concert treat is a night with Seamus Heaney and Liam O'Flynn: 'The Piper and The Poet.' Together these two men weave their poetry and music as one. Listening to the context — when the poem was written or the tune composed — and linking the stories together was magical.

A farewell picnic tea at Herbert Park with Dublin friends and a last visit to the beach in Donnabate north of Dublin, with friends Rob and Anne and their family are fitted into the last week. Jec is packing to move into a flat near Harold's Cross, sad to be staying in Dublin and not returning with us. I am planning one more walk across the cobblestones of Trinity to the Book of Kells, and a final wander up and down Grafton Street.

What an adventure we have had together. These 14 months in Ireland have changed us and given us another home to be in. We have learned the true meaning of the Irish proverb, "*Nil aon tintean mar do thintean Féin* — there is no place like home". *Sláinte! Go raimh maith agat.*

A FINAL KIWI UPDATE, AUGUST

Hannah surprises me by phoning me at work this morning, and Josh rings briefly too... just to say how excited they are that we will be home soon. Jude emails from Queenstown saying he and his Scottish friend Julie will arrive the day after we get home. Alice is trying to study for her final school exams amid the excitement of our return, the school ball season and waiting for the birth of Roze and Josh's first baby.

It will be spring as we step off the plane — my favourite season!

EPILOGUE

It has been a whirlwind ten days as we attempt to settle back into life at Sunshine Bay. The weather has been freezing; there is snow on the Orongorongo peaks behind us. We have been wishing for the warmth above the tanning shop on Bachelors Walk in Dublin again, and I have had to immediately unpack our Irish woollen jerseys. We are slowly setting up our home again, beside Wellington harbour this time, not the Liffey.

Today, however, is a stunning spring day in September. I have lunch outside on the deck and go for a walk. The young ones are jumping off the wharf at Days Bay, a sure sign that summer is looming, although the water must be icy. The house is full of spring flowers and there are cards everywhere: welcome home cards, my 50th birthday cards and, most special of all, cards to celebrate grandparenthood and the arrival of our new family member, Eddina Ruby Doherty. Eddina ('Eddie' already) was born early, just a week before my birthday and two days after we arrived home. She looks familiar. Josh and Roze are relaxed, mellow parents with a settled baby, who has already brought enormous joy to us all.

I celebrate being 50 with friends and family at a champagne breakfast on the deck. Gifts have arrived, beginning of course with Eddina Ruby. Others include a bowl from my sisters made of West Coast Buller River rocks, and Marie leaves a book under my pillow about all sorts of grandmas, including those with big wobbly bottoms and those who march in demonstrations.

Another friend sends a sex manual written by two Irish priests, "in case you hadn't seen it on sale in Ireland,". All the pages are blank!

Jessica, sitting beside Molly Malone at the end of Grafton Street, phones to wish me happy birthday.

We talk non-stop about Ireland, Donegal and Dublin. As our feet start to touch the ground here, the experiences of the last 18 months of planning, living and now absorbing our Irish experience, are already becoming part of our history. I find myself on the bus in motorway traffic with a huge grin on my face recalling some particular Irish moment or experience. Jack and I begin most of our conversations with, "Do you remember that day we saw/heard/felt …?"

I even manage to listen to talkback radio, and laugh out loud to hear them discussing where to buy the best meat pies in New Zealand. A more serious topic upsetting listeners is that of a motorway project that may need diverting around a taniwha. In Ireland the same debates revolve around the dells where fairies live. Town planners are slow learners, and ancient beliefs and traditions deserve respect and an appropriate response.

When we decided to go to Ireland for a period longer than a two-week holiday, I was advised to identify some 'tent pegs' to put down on arrival. My sturdy ones that I would leave behind in New Zealand had allowed me to pitch my tent on many a surface and in all sorts of weather. I wrote a list of the tent pegs I would put into the ground in Donegal. The list was small and included Jack and Alice, a roof over our heads, income from employment, access to email, a local newspaper to get my bearings and one or two Kiwi visitors to look forward to. All of these played a part in securing the Irish tent, and we weathered a few rough and windy patches together.

From the beginning, Jack, Alice and I were dependent on each other for stability and security, especially when we arrived homesick and fretting for those left behind. The welcome in Dublin from the Devlins, and the way the Kelly cousins prepared a home and space for us to be in Letterkenny, Donegal, were the best of beginnings. Some Kiwis did turn up early on to explore Donegal with us, and later when we moved to Dublin, others came for a night or a week or even a month in the Shoebox.

Our eight weeks in Donegal exploring just about everywhere, and immersing ourselves in all the county could offer — especially in respect of Jack and his Doherty clan connections to Inishowen — became a strong platform for the months that followed in Dublin. Alice's early decision to return home brought a peace to the three of us, but sadness too. One of my sturdiest tent pegs needed to go! Although the farewells at Dublin airport left us all in a sorry state, her decision also released us to shift to Dublin for work, and our moving into the one-bedroom apartment by the Ha'penny Bridge after almost thirty years of marriage and family life was 'fintarstic', as they say in Dublin.

We enjoyed the fun of adjusting to the novelty and noise across the river in Temple Bar, and to living as just 'the two of us'. We were sustained and nurtured by friends, Helen and Kevin, Sarah, Emmett and Tricia and their children, Joseph and Siobhan, Lew and Jiff, and my cousin Christine. And Jec came and lived with us for six months. Kia ora koutou! We could not have survived without your aroha and support.

Now, 14 months later, we have packed up the tent in Ireland and come back home in New Zealand, I am reflecting on the Irish tent pegs I needed to remove. Some of the pegs that I didn't know or even dream of on arrival have become treasures, moving from the ground and remaining in my heart. Many, many people made our time in Ireland unforgettable.

Thank you, Jack for being a curious and courageous free thinker who embraces life and makes things happen. Your positive outlook is contagious, and your thirst for history and its influence on us today makes for a future of certainty and hope.

Thank you to our children Josh and Roze, Hannah and Michael, Jude, Jessica and Alice, for allowing your mum and dad to be the ones taking off to explore overseas. I am proud of the people you have grown to be.

To our families and friends both in New Zealand and Ireland who helped make the experience so memorable, thank you. Your love and support made it easier for us to feel so much at home in Ireland, the land of our ancestors.

Some of you gave us your blessing to come. Others gave us your blessing to return. Our experience of home in Ireland and Aotearoa New Zealand is magnified because of all of you. Some of this has I hope been captured in this book.

Glossary

MAORI		IRISH	
Aotearoa	New Zealand	Ans Seirbhís	Out of Service
Aroha	Love, compassion	Babbies	Babies
Haere ra	Goodbye, farewell	Bodhrán	Drum
	(to person leaving)	Céad Míle Fáilte	A hundred thousand
Haka	Traditional Maori		welcomes
	posture dance	Ceileigh	Dance
Harakeke	Flax plant used for	Craic	Fun, good time,
	weaving		great talking
Iwi	Tribe	Currach	Traditional boat
Karakia	Prayer		used for fishing
Kia ora koutou	Greetings to you all	Desprit	Desperate, awful!
Korero	Talk or 'a chat'	Eejit	Idiot, fool
Korowai	Cloak	Feck	(fecked, fecky, etc)
Maori	Indigenous people		Politer use of F word
	of New Zealand		— used for just
Marae	Traditional gathering		about everything!
	place	Fianna Fáil	Political party,
Mihi	Speech or ceremony		currently in power
	of welcome	Gaeltacht	Designated areas of
Paua	Abalone shell		Ireland where Irish is
Pounamu	Jade stone found in		spoken
	New Zealand rivers	Garda	Irish police
Tangata whenua	'people of the land'	Go raibh maith agat	Thank you
	— the indigenous	Gossoon	Lad
	people	Mammys	Mothers
Te Wakaiti	'little canoe', a	Shanachie	Story teller
	community farm in	Sinn Féin	Republican political
	Wairarapa		party
Turangawaewae	A place to stand	Sláinte	Cheers!
	— your clan's land		
Waiata	Song		
Whakapapa	Genealogy		
Whanau	Family		

Mind Y'self Now, Jewarne

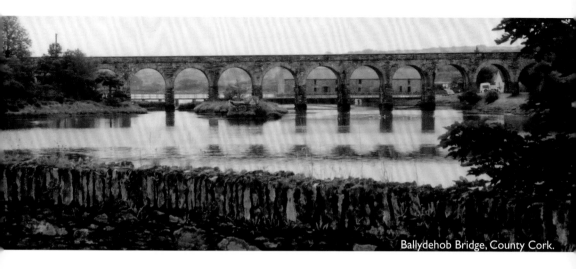

Ballydehob Bridge, County Cork.

INDEX

This is a selective index, mainly of places, and does not include family and friends, except in a few cases. Donegal and Dublin themselves are not indexed, as they are found throughout the book.

A

Adams, Gerry 55, 93
Ahern, Bertie 104
All Blacks 21, 42, 46, 51, 56, 71, 99–100, 103, 147, 155–6, 160, 173
Anna Livia 81–3, 93
Annascoul 170
Aotearoa Wall 87
Ardara 39, 55–6, 132, 165
Ardoyne 55–6
Ardrishaig 140–1, 143
Arlington pub 76, 99, 107, 124, 135
Armagh 73, 85, 174
Ash Wednesday 122, 125
Assisi 147
Átha Cliath 82
Athenry 44, 52, 71, 77, 79, 91, 106, 125, 161

B

Bachelors Walk 68–9, 74, 76, 78, 90, 92, 107, 117, 141, 152, 167, 182

Ballybofey 45
Ballydehob 177–8, 187
Ballyvourney 93, 180
Balor 48–9
Bantry Bay 113
Barry, Kevin 89, 96
Behan, Brendan 117
Belfast 30–1, 35, 43–4, 55, 71, 87, 92, 118
Binchy, Maeve 178
Black, Mary 14, 92, 94
Blair, Tony 26, 58
Blake, Peter 105, 109
Blessington 70, 118
Bloody Sunday 55, 57–9, 120
Boa Island 38–9
Bono 25–6, 103
Book of Kells 135, 181
Boyne Valley 129, 158, 164
Bray 70, 95, 152
Brosnan, Pierce 104–6
Bunbeg 49
Buncrana 18–19, 24, 28, 45–6, 60, 64, 74, 132, 165

Burke, Helen 9, 10, 61–2, 68, 75, 78, 88, 94, 97–8, 109, 123, 137, 150, 161, 177–9, 183
Burt Castle 18, 27, 132
Bushmills 32

C

Caherciveen 170
Caldragh 38–9
Callin 138
Campbell, Michael 154, 171
Cardiff 126–8; Cardiff Castle 126–7
Carndonagh 46
Carrick-on-Shannon 131
Carrickbraghy Castle 22, 29–31, 132
Carrickmacross 11, 14
Catherine of Aragon 126
Catholicism 12, 18–19, 43, 45, 47, 55, 57–8, 65, 78, 94, 109, 117–18, 120, 125, 132, 142, 146
Cavan 85, 164, 170
Chieftains, the 166
Clachan Mor 15, 42, 50
Clare, County 11, 14, 124, 134–6, 154, 163, 169
Clifden 168
Cliffs of Moher 133, 136, 169
Clonakilty 177
Cobh 171, 176
Collins, Michael 96, 177, 180
Colmcille 23, 36, 46, 56, 174, 179
Confirmation Day 94

Connemara 114, 116, 167
Cork 123, 156, 170–1, 176; Cork, County, 187
Croagh Patrick 176
Crookhaven 178
Culloden 139
Culmore 22

D

Dalkey 70, 164, 172
Deaker, Murray 147
Derg, Lough 166
Derry 8, 17–18, 22–3, 29, 44, 53, 57, 59, 64, 71, 74, 120, 131, 157, 159, 164–5, 170; Derry, County 11, 30, 74
Devenish Island 65, 131
Dingle 170–1
Doagh Island 29
Doheny & Nesbitts Pub 91
Doherty, Father Barney 13, 114–15
Doherty Keep 17–8, 45, 60, 64, 74, 132, 165
Donegal Castle 17, 41
Donovan (band) 92
Doolin 132–3, 135, 168–9
Doon Rock 18, 22–4, 45, 49
Down, County 173–4
Downings 71–2
Downpatrick 71, 174
Down Under Bar 102–3, 122, 173
Droitwich 126
Drombeg 177–8
Drumkeerin 131
Dublin Bay 62, 68, 96, 109, 111, 113
Dublin Castle 22, 76, 135
Dubliners, the (band) 97, 110, 164
Dublin Horse Fair 157
Dungloe 51
Dunluce Castle 32
Dunmore East 171

E

Earn, Loch 138
Edinburgh 93, 129, 137–8, 141, 175
Effin 123

Supporting Ireland in the World Cup.

Enniskillen 65, 73, 157
Erne, Lough 65, 131
Errigal, Mount 50, 52, 73

F

Famine Statues 79
Fanad Head 45
Featherston 12, 30, 32, 35, 87, 108, 113, 122, 139
Fermanagh, County 11, 38, 42, 65, 114–15, 131, 154, 175–6
Fianna Fáil 90
Firenze (Florence) 147, 150
Football World Cup 155
Foyle, Loch 17

G

Gaeltacht 19, 185
Gallaher, Dave 21
Galway 25, 51, 60, 71, 102, 114, 120, 132–3, 168, 175, 192
Gap of Mamore 28, 45, 132
Gartan 7, 23, 36-8; Gartan, Lough 7, 36
Giant's Causeway 32
Glasnevin 89, 96
Glencolumbcille 17, 36, 39–40
Glendalough 70, 72, 150, 164–5, 173
Glenties 17, 165
Glen Veagh evictions 37
Glen Veagh National Park 23
Grace, Patricia 21
Greencastle 30, 32, 132
Greystones 95, 152
Grianán of Aileach 4, 17–19, 60, 72–3, 131, 164–5
Guinness 75–6, 87, 93, 99–100, 135, 159

H

Ha'penny Bridge 14, 69, 74, 78, 107, 109, 127–8, 137, 183
H Block 43–4, 85–7
Heaney, Seamus 181
Hiruharama 14
Holy Hill 152, 166, 168
Holyrood Castle 138
Howth 95–6, 158, 164

I

Inch Castle 22, 29
Inch Island 17
Inishowen Peninsula 17–18, 22, 24, 29, 42, 45, 47, 63, 132, 183
Inverness 138–9
Irvinestown 38, 49, 65, 72, 131, 175–6
Italy 128, 144–5, 147, 149–50, 152–3, 160

J

Jamesons 93
Joyce, James 93, 96
Janus Stone 39

K

Kavanagh, Chris 97
Keane, JB 142
Keane, Roy 155–6
Kerry, County 47, 152, 161, 171; Kerry, Ring of 170
Kilcrohane 179
Kildare, County 61, 82, 111, 171
Kilkeel 175
Killarney 170, 179
Killideas 65
Killybegs 17, 39
Kilmacrennan 16, 24, 43, 45
Kilmainham Jail 8, 75, 124
Kilmartin 141
Knock 132
Kylemore Abbey 167–8

L

Larkin, James 34
Leitrim 11, 131, 154, 175
Letterkenny 7–8, 14–17, 19–21, 23–4, 26, 29, 31, 35–7, 41, 46, 48, 50–2, 63–5, 73, 79, 94, 132, 165, 183
Limerick 103–4, 180
Lismore 139–41
Literary Pub Crawl 101
Lochgilphead 140
Lomu, Jonah 51, 100, 103, 105
Lord of the Rings 107–8
Lucca 150
Lunney, Donal 85

M

McCool, Finn 32
MacGowan, Shane 110
McGuinness, Martin 8
Maguire's Castle 65
Malahide 107
Malin Head 28–9, 45, 132
Mayo, County 166–7
Meath, County 8, 34, 73, 159
Melmore Head 71
Mizen Head 178
Molly Malone 34, 63, 93, 159, 182
Monaghan, County 11
Moore, Christy 90, 92, 95, 179
Morrison, Van 92, 104
Mourne, mountains of 174
Muckross 167
Mull of Kintyre 30

N

Navan Fort 174
Newgrange 8, 33–5, 124, 129, 150, 164–5
New Zealand Ireland Association 70, 77, 105, 108, 122
Niall of the Nine Hostages 17

O

O'Connell Bridge 14, 119, 135
O'Connell, Daniel 93, 96
O'Connor, Mairtin 46
O'Connor, Sinead 92, 117, 159
O'Doherty, Sir Cahir 18, 22–5, 29
O'Flynn, Liam 181
O'Leary, Olivia 68, 78, 178
O'Reillys 170, 173
O'Reilly Castle 164
O'Riordan, Marian 61, 75, 94, 156
Olsen, Teresea 10
Omagh 35
Our Lady's Children's Hospital 75

P

Padre Pio 29, 160
Paisley, Ian 8
Papawai Marae 122
Patrick's Purgatory 166
Pisa 149–50
Pogues, the (band) 51, 96–7, 107, 109–10
Portaferry 71
Portnoo 63
Portsalon 45

Q

Quin 14, 154, 163, 169

R

Ramelton 18, 21
Rathmullen 17, 45, 62
Reid, John 73
Robinson, Mary 9, 68, 78, 88, 107, 154–5, 178
Rome 145–7

S

San Casciano Val di Pesa 149
Sandymount 68, 111
San Gimignano 148, 150
San Pancrazio 148, 150
Schull 88, 177–8, 180–1

A hungry Donegal donkey.

Scotland 8, 30–2, 36, 38, 64, 85, 87, 103, 105, 111, 127–8, 137–41, 153, 167
sex manual 182
Shelford, Buck 100, 147
Siena 146, 148, 150
Sinn Féin 8, 43, 55, 90, 107, 153, 185
Sistine Chapel 146–7
Skerries 173
Skibereen 177
Slane 129; Slane Abbey 130, 164; Slane Castle 25, 45, 129; Slane Hill 129
Sligo 132, 152, 166, 176
Spoleto 144, 147
St Blaise 117
St Brigid 117, 174; St Brigid's Well 133–4, 169
St Colmcille 23, 36, 174
St Stephen's Green 8, 95
St Eunan's cathedral 15, 27, 94
St Fechin 173
St James Hospital 75, 79, 90, 116, 156
St Kevin's cell 70, 164
St Molaise 115
St Patrick 18, 34, 71–2, 117, 121, 129, 135, 174
St Therese of Lisieux 94
Stirling Castle 138
Strabane 33
Stranford 71; Stranford, Lough 71
Sunshine Bay 11–12, 41–2, 87, 104, 143, 182
Swilly, Lough 17–18, 22, 45, 73

T

Tallaght Hospital 75, 88
Tara, Hill of 129
Taranaki, Mt 50
Tay, Loch 138–9
Temple Bar 7, 14, 34, 69, 74, 76, 99, 107, 141, 156–7, 159, 183
Temple Street Children's Hospital 75, 95
Te Wakaiti 12, 41–2, 84, 113, 162, 185
Thatcher, Margaret 43
Toibin, Niall 117
Tone, Wolfe 18
Tory Island 48–9, 51, 73
Toscana (Tuscany) 148, 150
Tramore Strand 39–40
Treaty of Waitangi 35, 57, 122–3
Trim 164
trinity, the female 117
Trinity College 8, 107, 171

U

University of Dublin 154
Uprising (1916) 85, 89, 169

V

Valencia Island 170
Vatican 146

W

Waitangi Day 122–3
Wallace Monument 138
Waterford 11, 122, 171
West Cork 9, 88, 94, 176–8, 181
Westmeath, County 173–4
Westport 14, 155, 166–7, 175–6
Whanganui River 14
Wicklow 70, 161; Wicklow Mountains 82, 118; Wicklow, County 61, 111, 165
Wilde, Oscar 93
Woods, Donald 53

Y

Youghal 171

Sunset, Galway Bay.

www.JoanneDoherty.co.nz
for more information or additional copies of this book.